Margaret

THE
WICKED WIT OF
PRINCESS
MARGARET

THE
WICKED WIT OF
PRINCESS
MARGARET

Compiled, edited
and introduced by

Karen Dolby

Michael O'Mara Books Limited

First published in Great Britain in 2018 by
Michael O'Mara Books Limited
9 Lion Yard
Tremadoc Road
London SW4 7NQ

A CIP catalogue record for this book is
available from the British Library.

Papers used by Michael O'Mara Books Limited are natural,
recyclable products made from wood grown in sustainable
forests. The manufacturing processes conform to the
environmental regulations of the country of origin.

ISBN 978-1-78243-958-5 in hardback print format
ISBN 978-1-78243- 959-2 in e-book format

1 3 5 7 9 10 8 6 4 2

Designed and typeset by Tetragon, London
Printer and bound by CPI Group (UK) Ltd, Croydon, CRO 4YY

www.mombooks.com

Contents

Introduction

*'I cannot imagine anything more
wonderful than to be who I am.'*

In June 2006, 896 items from Princess Margaret's private collection went under the hammer at Christie's auction house in London. Highlights included the Poltimore Tiara she wore for her wedding, countless gifts of Fabergé, furniture and jewels from her grandmother, Queen Mary, a gold and sapphire cigarette case from her father, King George VI, engraved with: 'To Margaret from her very devoted Papa GR Christmas 1949'. Other works of art: gifts and personal messages, from the simple to the most valuable, from family, friends, the public, organisations and heads of state, were also amongst the collection, which began in the Princess's childhood and archived her whole life. Like Princess Diana, with whom she was often compared, Princess Margaret had lived her life in the spotlight, her every move recorded and documented. She courted controversy and was fêted and photographed, praised and vilified, in equal measure.

Watching film footage of Princess Margaret, reading the anecdotes and conflicting accounts of her life, her character remains something of an enigma. Vivacious, charming and witty, she was also sometimes downright rude. A bohemian who was also a stickler for protocol. A snob who mixed widely.

So many contradictions. It's hard to escape the impression that sometimes the Princess behaved badly just because she could; a childhood instinct for naughtiness that never left her. As an adult she was often tempted to see just how far she could go and exactly how much she could get away with.

Bored, underemployed, not sufficiently challenged. Margaret was often let down by so-called friends. Her restless character needed a purpose and a role. When her beloved father died, she was stranded. Not only grieving and bereft, she watched as all around her family members took on new roles and important functions; everyone else's positions changed except for her own.

Writer and man of letters Gore Vidal, who came to know Princess Margaret well, commented, 'She was far too intelligent for her station in life … She often had a bad press, the usual fate of wits in a literal society.'

Hers was a strange position. Born fourth in line to the throne, she went up to third at the age of six, when her uncle abdicated, then back down to fourth again in 1948 with the birth of Prince Charles, after which she continued dropping. She was number eleven at the time of her death in 2002.

Unlike her elder sister, Elizabeth, Margaret's role was not defined. She had no fixed path and as a result vascillated between duty and inclination. She was drawn to the arts and artists of all sorts, but she was also royalty in a world where the old order was changing. She chose to mix in a society where rank and birth no longer held sway but for someone like the Princess, this was a contradictory mix. She was ever aware of her position and even when most relaxed and uninhibited would sometimes step back and pull rank. Throughout, Princess Margaret's life bore witness to the big question that *The Guardian* posed in its obituary of her – 'what, exactly, is a princess for?'

From glamorous style icon to a rather lonely figure; in ill-health and semi-paralysed, living out her days at Kensington Palace, Princess Margaret was always her own woman. Fêted by the press in her youth as the beautiful, tragic Princess who sacrificed love for duty, she was equally criticised in her later years for her icy hauteur and difficult demands.

Close friends remember a loyal, fun-loving woman who was frequently misunderstood.

She could be utterly preposterous, rude, demanding and outrageous. She could also be warm, witty and clever. There was no excuse for some of her behaviour but she could never be accused of being boring. And there was something about Princess Margaret that kept friends, enemies and everyone in between, entranced.

This book focuses on her unique wit and sharp view of society and the world, told through her own words and stories from those who knew her best.

Timeline
of Princess Margaret's Life

1930   Princess Margaret Rose is born on 21 August 1930 at Glamis Castle in Scotland, to Elizabeth Bowes-Lyon, Duchess of York, and Prince Albert, Duke of York. Her birth is not registered for several days to avoid her being number 13 on the parish register. Her mother initially wants to call her Ann Margaret, but her father dislikes the name Ann. They decide upon Margaret Rose instead. The family live at 145 Piccadilly in London.

1932   Her parents make Royal Lodge in Windsor Great Park their country home.

1936   King Edward VIII abdicates on 11 December in order to marry divorcee Wallis Simpson. His brother, Margaret's father, becomes King George VI and her elder sister Elizabeth becomes heir to the throne.

1939   The Second World War is declared on 1 September while the princesses are at Birkhall on the Balmoral estate. They remain here until Christmas, which they spend at Sandringham House, and then move to Windsor Castle where they are to remain for most of the war. Prime

Minister Winston Churchill advises the evacuation of both princesses to Canada. The Queen Mother famously replies, 'The children won't go without me. I won't leave the King. And the King will never leave.'

1940 On 13 October, Margaret joins her sister to make her first public broadcast on *Children's Hour* on BBC radio.

1944 Wing Commander Peter Townsend is appointed Equerry to King George VI (he does not become Group Captain until the beginning of 1953).

1945 The Second World War ends. Princess Margaret appears on the balcony at Buckingham Palace with her family and Prime Minister Winston Churchill. Later, she and Elizabeth join the celebrating crowds outside the Palace gates.

1946 Princess Margaret is confirmed into the Church of England on 15 April.

1947 Margaret embarks on her first trip abroad on 1 February; a three-month state tour of Southern Africa with her parents and sister. The Princess is chaperoned by Peter Townsend. On 9 July, Princess Elizabeth's engagement to Prince Philip of Greece and Denmark is announced. Margaret is a bridesmaid at their wedding on 20 November at Westminster Abbey.

1948 The Princess carries out her first royal duty overseas in September, attending the inauguration of Queen Juliana of the Netherlands. Margaret's first nephew, Prince Charles, is born on 14 November. The number of Princess Margaret's official engagements increases. She begins to take on roles as Patron or President of various charities and other organisations.

1950   Margaret and Elizabeth's trusted former nanny Marion Crawford publishes *The Little Princesses*, a book of anecdotes about her time with the young princesses. This is seen as an unforgivable breach of trust and any future betrayals by those close to the Royal Family are referred to as 'doing a Crawfie'.

1951   Margaret's 21st birthday party is held at Balmoral in August. In September, her father George VI undergoes surgery for lung cancer. Princess Margaret is appointed as one of the Counsellors of State, undertaking royal duties while the King is ill.

1952   King George VI dies on 6 February. Princess Elizabeth is proclaimed Queen and returns from royal tour in Kenya. Princess Margaret and the Queen Mother move out of Buckingham Palace into apartments at Clarence House. Peter Townsend is appointed Comptroller of the Queen Mother's Household. He divorces his first wife, Rosemary Pawle.

1953   News of the relationship between Princess Margaret and Group Captain Peter Townsend becomes public after the Queen's coronation on 2 June. The couple ask the Queen for permission to marry. The Queen initially transfers Townsend from her mother's Household to her own. After continuing opposition from the Cabinet, Parliament and the Church, Winston Churchill arranges for Townsend to be posted to Brussels for two years.

1955   On 31 October, Princess Margaret issues a statement, ending the speculation and categorically saying that she will not be marrying the Group Captain. Undertaking an official tour of the West Indies, the Princess visits the Caribbean for the first time.

1958   Buckingham Palace issues a statement on 21 May, again denying an engagement between Princess Margaret and Peter Townsend after a report by the London correspondent appears in the *Tribune de Genève*. This follows several meetings between the pair that month, and a flurry of speculation. The couple say a final goodbye and are not to meet again for more than thirty years.

Also in May, Princess Margaret meets the photographer Antony Armstrong-Jones.

1959   In October, the Princess receives a letter from Townsend telling her that he is going to marry Marie-Luce Jamagne. In December, Margaret and Antony Armstrong-Jones become privately engaged.

1960   The Queen gives her formal consent to Margaret's marriage in January. On 26 February, the Queen Mother issues the formal announcement of the engagement of Princess Margaret to Antony Armstrong-Jones. The wedding takes place at Westminster Abbey on 6 May. It is the first royal wedding to be televised. The couple's honeymoon is a six-week tour of the Caribbean on board the royal yacht *Britannia*. On their return, the couple move into an apartment at 10 Kensington Palace. The Princess is offered a plot of land on the island of Mustique by her friend Colin Tennant, as a wedding present.

1961   On 6 October, Antony Armstrong-Jones is made Earl of Snowdon and Viscount Linley of Nymans in the County of Sussex. On 3 November, the couple's first child is born, David Albert Charles Armstrong-Jones, 2nd Earl of Snowdon, known as Viscount Linley.

1963   The Snowdons move into their newly refurbished home in March: the much larger, four-storey, twenty-room apartment at 1A Clock Court, Kensington Palace. This is to remain the Princess's home for the rest of her life.

1964 The couple's second child, Lady Sarah Frances Elizabeth Armstrong-Jones, is born on 1 May at Kensington Palace.

1968 Princess Margaret revisits Mustique and marks out the ten-acre plot for her house there.

1973 The Princess moves into her villa on Mustique. It is named '*Les Jolies Eaux*'. At a house party in Scotland, Princess Margaret is introduced to Roddy Llewellyn.

1976 In February, photographs of the Princess and Roddy Llewellyn wearing swimsuits at a beach on Mustique appear in the press. Lord Snowdon moves out of the family home. On 19 March, it is announced that the couple have agreed to formally separate. At this time it is said there are no plans to divorce.

1978 In early May, Princess Margaret is admitted to the King Edward VII Hospital in London suffering from hepatitis. On 10 May, it is announced that Princess Margaret and Lord Snowdon will divorce. The Princess leaves hospital on 11 May, as part of her cure, she is not to drink alcohol for a year.

On 11 July, the decree absolute on the Princess's divorce is granted.

In September, the Princess is taken ill during a tour of the South Pacific. She is hospitalised with viral pneumonia. On 15 December, Lord Snowdon marries Lucy Lindsay-Hogg.

1981 Prince Charles marries Lady Diana Spencer on 29 July at St Paul's Cathedral.

Roddy Llewellyn marries Tatiana Soskin, with Princess Margaret's blessing.

1985 On 5 January, the Princess undergoes a serious operation at the Brompton Hospital in London, in which part of her left lung is removed. Lung cancer is feared but the growth proves benign.

1986 Prince Andrew marries Sarah Ferguson in July.

1992 Princess Margaret and Peter Townsend meet for lunch at Kensington Palace in the summer. They have not seen one another for thirty-four years. It is their final meeting. The Duke and Duchess of York separate after embarrassing photographs of the Duchess appear in the press. The separation of the Prince and Princess of Wales is announced in December.

1993 In January, Princess Margaret is taken ill with pneumonia.
On 8 October, Viscount Linley marries Serena Alleyne Stanhope.

1994 On 14 July, Lady Sarah Armstrong-Jones marries Daniel Chatto.
Prince Charles admits to his relationship with Camilla Parker Bowles in an authorised biography and television interview.

1995 Princess Diana appears in her 'Queen of Hearts' *Panorama* interview on BBC TV. Peter Townsend dies on 19 June 1995. Buckingham Palace issues a statement that Princess Margaret is 'saddened by the news'.

1996 Princess Margaret's first grandchild is born on 28 July, her daughter Sarah's son, Samuel Chatto.

1997 On 31 August, Princess Diana dies after a road accident in Paris. Her funeral takes place on 6 September.

1998   Princess Margaret suffers a mild stroke but appears to make a good recovery.

1999   The Princess is severely scalded in the shower at her home on Mustique. The resulting burns to her feet never properly heal and affect her mobility.

David Linley's first child is born on 1 July: Charles Patrick Inigo Armstrong-Jones. Sarah Chatto's second son Arthur is born.

2001   Early in the year, further strokes leave the Princess semi-paralysed and with partial vision. She makes a public appearance at her mother's 101st birthday celebration in August. Her final public appearance is in December at the 100th birthday celebration of her aunt, Princess Alice, Duchess of Gloucester.

2002   On 9 February, it is announced that Princess Margaret has died at the King Edward VII Hospital in London after another stroke. She was seventy-one.

Sisters and Daughters

Princess Margaret Rose was born at Glamis Castle, her mother's ancestral home, during a raging storm, on the evening of 21 August 1930. She was the first royal to be born in Scotland for 300 years and the last whose birth had to be legally witnessed by the Home Secretary to verify she was a genuine royal baby. As the second daughter of the Duke and Duchess of York, she was fourth in line to the throne.

Her early years were spent mainly in the York's London townhouse at 145 Piccadilly and Royal Lodge Windsor, but life changed completely when her father became King George VI after the abdication of her uncle, Edward VIII, in December 1936.

The new King and his family moved into Buckingham Palace and Margaret was given a bedroom overlooking the Mall. She found the long, draughty corridors and hundreds of rooms, echoing and unfriendly. With their parents otherwise occupied, the young princesses spent an increasing amount of time with nurses and their nanny and governess, Marion Crawford, usually known as Crawfie.

Always a precocious child, and a fast learner, as a baby Princess Margaret began to hum the waltz from *The Merry Widow*. Her maternal grandmother, Lady Strathmore, who was carrying Margaret as an infant down stairs on one of these occasions said, 'I was so astounded that I almost dropped her.'

Although their parents were at pains to protect their young daughters from the growing constitutional crisis and gossip about King Edward VIII – or Uncle David as he was known to the girls – some of the rumours must have reached their ears. When a puzzled Princess Margaret asked her elder sister what all the fuss was about and why Prime Minister Baldwin was constantly visiting their home at 145 Piccadilly, Elizabeth replied, 'I think Uncle David wants to marry Mrs Baldwin and Mr Baldwin doesn't like it.'

It was Crawfie who broke the news to her charges that their Papa was to be King and they were to move to Buckingham Palace. At the age of six, Margaret at first was more concerned about their name change: 'I have only just learned how to spell York and now I am not to use it any more. I am to sign myself Margaret all alone.'

The change meant that the princesses were to see a lot less of their parents. In view of this, King George had two large rocking horses placed outside his office so that he could hear his daughters rocking to and fro while he worked.

After their father's coronation in 1937, seven-year-old Margaret asked if this meant Elizabeth would have to be the next Queen. When her older sister nodded, 'Yes, someday,' Margaret commiserated, 'Poor you.'

With Elizabeth being groomed as the heir to the throne, Margaret felt increasingly left behind.

'Now that Papa is King, I am nothing,' she said.

King George in particular was concerned that she shouldn't feel relegated to the background as the younger 'spare' – as he had been as a child. As a result, Margaret was often over-indulged by her parents and she could be wilful and competitive.

The daughter of one of the Palace courtiers at the time claimed, 'She was his [George VI] pet ... she was always allowed to stay up to dinner at the age of thirteen and to grow up too quickly.'

When talking about his daughters, the King described Elizabeth as his pride and Margaret as his joy. He also said of his youngest daughter, 'She is able to charm the pearl out of an oyster.'

Margaret could always make her father laugh, even when he was trying to tell her off, interrupting him on one occasion to ask, 'Papa, do you sing, "God Save My Gracious Me"?'

A Royal Childhood

Growing up, the princesses were close, although four years apart in age. They enjoyed singing showtunes together, with Margaret playing the piano. Both laughed at the same jokes and were good mimics, though Margaret's wit was sharper and less gentle than her older sister's.

Their cousin Margaret Rhodes wrote, 'Princess Margaret was the naughty one. She was always more larky. She used to tease the servants. There was a wonderful old page and, as he carried the plates around the dining room, Margaret used to stare at him, trying to make him laugh. But she never got herself reprimanded. She got away with everything.'

The young Margaret also had an imaginary friend named Cousin Halifax, who was given the blame for many of her 'little troubles'.

'I was busy with Cousin Halifax,' she would say to explain why some task had been overlooked.

Not that some members of staff weren't tempted to tell her off. One Palace courtier remembered, 'There were moments when I'd have given anything to have given her the hell of a slap.' Another commented simply, 'She was a wicked little girl.'

Favourite tricks were to jump out from behind pillars on unsuspecting Palace staff and to replace sugar with salt. Royal nanny, Crawfie, wrote, 'More than once I have seen an equerry put his hand into his pocket, and find it, to his amazement, full of sticky lime balls ... Shoes left outside doors would become inexplicably filled with acorns.'

'Isn't it lucky that Lilibet's the eldest,' Margaret said, alluding to the fact that Elizabeth was always better behaved.

Crawfie described Margaret as a practical joker, 'a born comic' who could be disruptive, fond of 'light-hearted fun and frolics ... amusing and outrageous ... antics.'

The 1950 publication of Marion Crawford's memoir *The Little Princesses* horrified the royal family and she was ever after ostracised and ignored by them. As the Queen Mother warned her in a letter before the book was published, anyone connected with the family was expected to remain loyal: 'people in positions of trust with us must be utterly oyster'.

After the book appeared in print, the Queen Mother wrote, 'We have worried greatly over this matter, and can only think that our late and completely trusted governess has gone off her head ...'

Princess Margaret later said of her old nanny, 'She sneaked.'

Elizabeth was five and Margaret two when Crawfie first arrived. She was aware of the persistent, unfounded rumours circulating that Margaret could neither speak nor hear, 'A notion not without humour to those who knew her.' As an adult, Margaret herself reflected that she had been 'a chatty child'.

Viewed today, Crawfie's reminiscences in her memoir seem fairly affectionate and innocent. But the book attracted a great deal of interest in its time, particularly for its portrayal of the contrasting characters of the two girls and its hints at the difficulties that might lie ahead for Margaret.

Crawfie asserted: 'Margaret was a great joy and a diversion ... Lilibet was the one with the temper but it was under control. Margaret was often naughty, but she had a gay bouncing way with her which was hard to deal with. She would often defy me with a sidelong look, make a scene and kiss and be friends and all forgiven and forgotten.'

Crawfie also noted of 'Lilibet': 'All her feeling for her pretty sister was motherly and protective. She hated Margaret to be left out; she hated her antics to be misunderstood … How often in early days have I heard her cry in real anguish, "Stop her, Mummy. Oh, please stop her" when Margaret was being more than usually preposterous and amusing and outrageous. Though Lilibet, with the rest of us, laughed at Margaret's antics – and indeed it was impossible not to – I think they often made her uneasy and filled her with foreboding.'

Keen to delay the day's lessons, Margaret used various tactics, often stories of her 'appalling' dreams.

'Crawfie, I must tell you an amazing dream I had last night.' Both governess and older sister would listen, 'as the account of green horses, wild-elephant stampedes, talking cats and other remarkable manifestations went into two or three instalments.' Margaret had a real talent for acting and mimicry. 'The gift of fun-poking – and very clever fun-poking – kept her listeners in fits of slightly uneasy laughter.'

The former governess thought older people were often frightened of Margaret. 'She had too witty a tongue and too sharp a way with her, and I think they one and all felt they would probably be the next on her list of caricatures!'

Her talent for mimicry was one the Princess developed over the years. In 1949, writer and historian James Lees-Milne recorded in his June diary his friend and fellow writer James Pope-Hennessy's comment that the nineteen-year-old Margaret was 'high spirited to the verge of indiscretion. She mimics Lord Mayors welcoming her on platforms and crooners on the wireless, in fact anyone you care to mention.'

Like most sisters, the princesses could also fight – Elizabeth was apparently 'quick with her left hook', while Margaret was 'known to bite on occasions'. Elizabeth often complained, 'Margaret always wants everything I want.' However, by nature rather more quiet and shy than her younger sister, Elizabeth was equally keen for Margaret to be invited along to parties and social events too, explaining, 'Oh, it's so much easier when Margaret's there – everybody laughs at what Margaret says.'

The young Elizabeth also tried to offer her sister guidance on the right way to behave. 'If you see someone with a funny hat, Margaret, you must not point at it and laugh.'

> When a rather chubby visitor arrived at the
> Palace, the young Princess Margaret prodded
> his stomach and asked, 'Is that *all* of you?'

Dressed as an angel and about to set off to a fancy dress party, her mother regarded her younger daughter and said, 'You don't look very angelic, Margaret.' Without hesitation Margaret replied cheerfully, 'That's all right. I'll be a holy terror.'

At another party aged six, Margaret prayed fervently that the conjuror entertainer would not call her up onto the stage. He did not and she later claimed, 'That childish experience gave me confidence in the power of prayer, which I've believed in ever since.'

Assured as a child that nothing was impossible if you tried hard enough, the Princess was unconvinced, pointing out, 'Have you ever tried putting toothpaste back into its tube?'

When the nine-year-old Margaret was reunited with her parents after their state visit to the US and Canada, she was proud to show her mother how she had lost weight while they were away, exclaiming, 'Look, Mummy, I am quite a good shape now, not like a football like I used to be.'

The Queen Mother had been keen to call her younger daughter 'Ann', but George VI did not like the name. Still, Margaret later quizzed her parents, 'You gave Lilibet three names [Elizabeth Alexandra Mary]. Why didn't you give me three instead of only two? Margaret Rose!'

The young princesses Elizabeth and Margaret were not allowed to mix very widely with other children, but an exception was made for the Girl Guides, and in 1937 the 1st Buckingham Palace Company of Guides was formed. Soon afterwards, eleven-year-old Elizabeth requested that seven-year-old Margaret also be allowed to join as a Brownie, explaining, 'You see, she does so love getting dirty.'

The resulting pack comprised around twenty Guides and fourteen Brownies, all carefully selected, well-connected daughters of Palace employees and court officials. Their headquarters was a summerhouse in the gardens of Buckingham Palace. The girls were associated with a Balmoral Company unit while their own closed temporarily during World War II.

Camping out at night, loud giggles could always be heard coming from the young Princess Margaret's tent. These were temporarily suppressed when the girls were told to be quiet by the company leader, only to be replaced by even more raucous laughter as Margaret mimicked the telling off.

Nevertheless, Margaret was a keen Brownie and Guide. At thirteen she wrote to her grandmother, Queen Mary, 'I am working for my needlewoman's badge. I have done hemming, gathers, a button hole, over-sewing and a darn. Then I have to do a patch on flannel and make a useful garment.'

War Years

Princess Margaret would often accompany her older sister as she carried out minor public duties during wartime Britain. Princess Elizabeth had been made Honorary Colonel in Chief of a regiment in 1942 and was also a member of the Auxiliary Transport Service or ATS. The press would always take photographs of them both, but invariably Margaret would find herself cropped from the picture when it actually appeared in print. This was largely for practical reasons because the newspapers themselves were drastically scaled down in size due to wartime shortages. Margaret would check and joke wryly, 'I've been censored again.'

When the Second World War broke out in 1939, the princesses were evacuated to Windsor Castle. Nine-year-old Margaret asked, 'Who is this Hitler spoiling everything?'

Margaret recalled, 'There was a tremendous spirit at Windsor. Everybody was always very cheerful.' The Princess also remembered the extra defences at the Castle: 'We were not allowed to go far from the house in case there were air raids; and there had been a pathetic attempt to defend the castle with trenches and some rather feeble barbed wire. It could not have kept anyone out, but it did keep us in.'

The Actress Princess

Each year just before Christmas, the princesses would take part in a pantomime held in the Waterloo Chamber at Windsor Castle. In 1941, it was *Cinderella*, with Elizabeth as a dashing Prince Florizel and Margaret as Cinderella. In 1943, they staged a more ambitious performance of *Aladdin*, which was very much Margaret's production. 'She produced drawings … she arranged all the parts. She talked pantomime constantly.'

It was Margaret who really enjoyed acting. Elizabeth tended to perform her roles rather more dutifully, but on the day of the pantomime it was always Margaret who, according to Crawfie, would wake up feeling sick and looking 'absolutely pea-green'.

Margaret would somehow manage to pull herself together and overcome her nerves. Even as a small girl she had played the part of the Little Child in the shepherd's hut and sang 'Gentle Jesus, Meek and Mild'. Crawfie recorded: 'She had a most beautifully clear voice, and she sang it all alone, with that great hall half-full of people.'

Letters to Crawfie

Writing to her governess from Windsor in 1943, Margaret gives an insight into her life at the Castle:

As you never write to me, I'm going to write to you. Ha! Ha! How are you? Did you have a happy Xmas? We did. Philip [the future Duke of Edinburgh] *came! On Xmas Eve we all had dinner together. There were only nine of us … Then after dinner, we put out all the lights and listened to a ghost story. We settled ourselves to be frightened – and were NOT. Most disappointing. Then we danced (on the little bits of board we could find) to the wireless as the gramophone wouldn't work.*

Then on Xmas night we had dinner together. The Bofors officers came. Quite nice. Then we rolled back the carpet and danced to the gramophone as it had been mended. Danced till one o'clock! …

Lilibet has a cold. Bother … With heaps, piles, mounds, mountains of love from Margaret.

Balmoral Summers

Margaret and Elizabeth's cousin, Margaret Rhodes, spent much of her childhood with the princesses and every summer she holidayed with them at Balmoral, usually staying at Birkhall on the estate. In her book *The Final Curtsey*, she remembered one year when the Grand Duchess Xenia, the exiled sister of the last Tsar of Russia, was staying at nearby Craigowan. Whenever the three cousins were anywhere near Craigowan, they would begin loudly singing the 'Volga Boatmen's Song'.

Margaret Rhodes recalls, 'We thought that the serenade would remind her of her homeland, but looking back I suppose our behaviour was less than sensitive, bearing in mind her tragic experiences during the revolution.'

Margaret Rhodes also recalled being kept awake by her younger cousin Margaret who had the bedroom next to hers at Birkhall. As they were supposedly going to sleep, the Princess would sing 'Old Macdonald had a Farm' over and over, complete with the appropriate animal noises. She was known to be afraid of the dark, so maybe this was her way of comforting herself.

It was the family's tradition to hold a Balmoral house party for the start of the grouse-shooting season, to which the same close circle of guests were always invited. Margaret Rhodes wrote how the cousins would sing the latest popular songs towards the end of the dinner. She added, 'When she was older, Princess Margaret, who had a satirical wit, would create topical new lyrics for these top-of-the-pops performances. She missed her vocation; she should have been in cabaret.'

A Tale of Two Sisters

By the time Margaret reached her mid teens she appeared 'mentally ahead of her age', according to her former governess, Crawfie. She seemed on a par with her older sister in years and definitely no longer very interested in school work. The pair had always had very different characters but now their differing interests began to appear more obvious.

Queen Mary's lady-in-waiting, Lady Airlie, visiting Sandringham for the first post-war Royal family Christmas there, was able to observe the differences in character between both princesses. Elizabeth was then nineteen and Margaret fifteen. In her opinion, no sisters, 'could have been less alike than the princesses, the elder with her quiet simplicity, the younger with her puckish expression and irrepressible high spirits – often liberated in mimicry.'

Princess Elizabeth loved to don a pair of her father's plus-fours and tramp the hills around Balmoral deerstalking with the King. This was not at all to Margaret's taste. She preferred indoor games like charades or canasta. Group Captain Peter Townsend described her playing cards of an evening shortly after the war's end, 'with so little respect for the seriousness of the game that each coup was accompanied either by loud groans or gales of laughter.'

Like the rest of her family, she did however like family picnics at Balmoral and loved galloping her horse across the estate. A former member of the household staff there described the sisters' contrasting riding styles, 'Elizabeth, on a horse, was competent and classic ... Margaret was pretty and dashing.'

> Margaret was known to describe her position in the royal hierarchy rather flippantly: 'I'm heir apparent to the heir presumptive.' The heir and the spare.
>
> This was obviously before her sister became Queen or had any children.

The Doting Young Aunt

After the birth of her first nephew, Prince Charles, in 1948, Princess Margaret quipped, 'I suppose I'll now be known as Charlie's Aunt.'

Single and just eighteen when her nephew was born, Margaret was a doting aunt. 'Darling Charles has been with us for a fortnight and is standing holding on to things at only nine months,' she wrote from Balmoral in summer 1949.

After the birth of her niece, Anne, a couple of years later she commented, 'The children get more and more angelic every day.' She laughed at their antics and recorded how after the Argyll pipers had played for them, 'Charles put on one of the huge feather bonnets the drummers wear! He completely disappeared.'

All Change

Shortly after Elizabeth's coronation as Queen in June 1953, Anne Tennant, one of Margaret's ladies-in-waiting, came upon the Princess looking sad and very tearful. 'I've lost my father and I've lost my sister,' Margaret explained. 'She will be busy. Our lives will change.'

However relaxed she might seem when socialising, the Princess never forgot her royal position and frequently pulled rank. One of her standard dinner party claims was, 'I am unique. I am the daughter of a king and the sister of a queen.'

A Royal Air

As an adult, should anyone refer to Elizabeth simply as her sister, Margaret was very quick to point out to them curtly, 'When you say my sister, I imagine you are referring to Her Majesty the Queen.'

She was equally strict if anyone mentioned her mother, correcting, 'Surely you mean Queen Elizabeth the Queen Mother.' When asked at a children's party, 'Is your mother well?' the Princess replied icily, '*Her Majesty* is very well, thank you.'

At a dinner party with writer and columnist A.N. Wilson, the subject turned to how often people in all walks of life dream of the Queen, and afterwards wake feeling a sense of peace and blessing, as if it was almost a quasi-religious experience. 'Quite right, too,' Margaret answered. 'After all, the Queen is God's representative in this realm.'

When author and friend Gore Vidal passed on to her Jackie Kennedy's opinion that she had found the Queen 'pretty heavy-going', Margaret was nonplussed. 'But that's what she's there for,' she explained.

Princess Margaret once commented, 'The Queen is the only person who can put on a tiara with one hand while walking downstairs.'

She could also put her sister in her place. Replying to the Queen's criticism of her flirtatious behaviour, Margaret told her curtly, 'You look after your empire and I'll look after my life.'

Talking about family, Margaret explained, 'In our family, we don't have rifts. We have a jolly good row and then it's all over and I've only twice ever had a row with my sister.' Intriguingly, she never confessed to what the two arguments were about.

Mothers and Daughters

Princess Margaret's relationship with her mother was not always an easy one, especially after the death of her beloved father when she and the Queen Mother both moved from Buckingham Palace to apartments in nearby Clarence House on the Mall. Although they lived one above the other, they often communicated by letter, few of which survive as Princess Margaret burned many of her mother's papers and letters during the 1990s. A process she described as 'doing a bit of sorting'.

William Shawcross, the Queen Mother's biographer, wrote of Princess Margaret: 'Even her closest friends could not predict when her mood might change from gaiety to hauteur. Although she loved her mother, she was not always kind to her – indeed she could be rude. On one occasion Lady Penn said to Queen Elizabeth, "I can't bear to see the way Princess Margaret treats you." To which Queen Elizabeth replied, "Oh, you mustn't worry about that. I'm quite used to it."' Lady Penn was a close family friend and contemporary of Elizabeth and Margaret.

Christopher Warwick, one of the Princess's biographers, wrote, 'The relationship between Queen Elizabeth [the Queen Mother] and Princess Margaret was almost stereotypically mother and daughter: each guaranteed at times to bait and irritate the other.'

> If she came upon her mother watching a television programme that she didn't like, Margaret would simply change channels. She criticised her mother's dress sense frequently and openly, asking, 'Why do you dress in those ridiculous clothes?'

The Princess was equally unimpressed by her mother's choice of homes. 'I can't think why you have such a horrible place as the Castle of Mey.' This was Margaret's verdict the only time she went to the Queen Mother's Scottish retreat in Caithness, on the north coast of Scotland, which she had bought in 1952, shortly after her husband George VI's death.

Bearing in mind that it had taken Margaret thirty years to actually visit the castle, her mother replied reasonably, 'Well, darling, you needn't come again.'

She was also critical of the architect who had been employed to work on her mother's ancestral home, Glamis Castle. 'I hear you've completely ruined my mother's old home,' she told the poor man. She compounded matters by asking, 'Have you ever looked at yourself in a mirror and seen the way you walk?' He had been disabled from birth.

Close friends tried to excuse her rudeness and cruelty. One said, 'I think she was trying to be cheeky. She thought she was trying to reach a kind of intimacy.'

Grannie Mary R and Grandpapa England

It was Elizabeth who nicknamed her grandfather King George V, 'Grandpapa England', Margaret was far less at ease with her grandparents than her parents. She once described George V as 'a most objectionable old man' and her grandmother Queen Mary as 'absolutely terrifying' adding, 'she didn't really like children and made no sort of effort with them.'

After being told that her grandfather the King had died, Margaret said, 'Grandpapa has gone to heaven and I am sure God is finding him very useful.'

Margaret was only five when George V died and she probably had few clear memories of him, but her grandmother was a formidable presence throughout her childhood and into her early twenties.

As an adult looking back, she told Gore Vidal, 'I detested Queen Mary. She was rude to all of us except Lilibet, who was going to be Queen. Of course, she had an inferiority complex. We were royal, and she was not.'

Although Mary was a great granddaughter of King George III and Princess of Teck, she was a Serene Highness at birth, rather than a Royal Highness like Margaret and Elizabeth. Margaret, with her keen sense of hierarchy, would have been very aware of the difference.

At the Christie's auction of Princess Margaret's private collection, the sheer number of gifts from Queen Mary to her granddaughter would suggest – at least at one time – a rather more warm and friendly relationship. Among these gifts were pieces of Art Deco diamond jewellery and jewelled, enamelled, glass Fabergé scent bottles along with many handwritten notes: 'For darling Margaret on her confirmation day from her loving Grannie Mary R, God Bless You, April 15th 1946' and, 'Fan which belonged to Queen Alexandra given her by her sister Marie Empress of Russia – given to Princess Margaret of York by her grandmother Queen Mary, 1932'.

As an adult remembering her grandmother's character, Princess Margaret observed, 'Queen Mary was one of those women who prefer male company. Although my mother always said that she was a wonderful mother-in-law, Queen Mary didn't really like other women. She would put herself out tremendously for men, and could be utterly charming.'

She also said of her formidably regal grandmother, 'She had such an image!'

Romance
and Rumour

By 1948, life was changing for Princess Margaret. At the beginning of the year she was still known as Margaret Rose. By the end of it she had dropped the 'Rose', perhaps to signify that she was no longer a child. Her older sister had married the year before and in November 1948 gave birth to her first child. King George VI was also beginning to suffer the ill-health that was to lead to his premature death four years later at the age of fifty-six. Princess Elizabeth, as his elder daughter and heir, was increasingly taking on his duties. Margaret had lost her companion at the Palace. She had begun to take on royal engagements but these were always the less important or exciting. Meanwhile, she was attracting growing personal attention.

The Royal Catch

The *Picture Post* of summer 1950 posed its readers the question: 'Is it her sparkle, her youthfulness, her small stature, or the sense of fun she conveys, that makes Her Royal Highness Princess Margaret the most sought-after girl in England? And this not only amongst her own set of young people but amongst all the teenagers who rush to see her in Norfolk and Cornwall, or wherever she goes.'

At the same time, Group Captain Peter Townsend, equerry to King George VI, and now promoted to assistant master of the royal household with a smart office in Buckingham Palace, noted of the young Princess, 'If her extravagant vivacity sometimes outraged the elder members of the household and of London society, it was contagious to those who still felt young.' He was then thirty-six, she was just twenty.

Rumours of their romance were to set press and public gossip alight. Rightly or wrongly, this was the affair that came to define Margaret as the tragic Princess who was forced to give up her true love. Endless speculation followed as to how different the course of her life might have been if she had been allowed to follow her heart. Princess Margaret has never written publicly about the relationship. She left it to others, notably Peter Townsend himself. It's obvious from his memoirs that more than her beauty, it was her wit, joy and humour that drew him to her.

Destiny's Daughter

In 1948, Duff Cooper, at the time Britain's ambassador to France, met the King and Queen together with the Princess in Paris. After their lunch he wrote in his diary, 'Margaret is a most attractive girl – lovely eyes, lovely mouth, very sure of herself and full of humour. She might get into trouble before she's finished.'

He was not the only person to have concerns for the vivacious young Princess. The diarist Henry 'Chips' Channon met her around the same time and wondered what the future would hold for her, noting, 'there is already a Marie-Antoinette aroma about her'.

Her famously dignified grandmother, Queen Mary, described her younger granddaughter as '*espiegle*' or 'mischievous' and rather uncharacteristically declared, 'She is so outrageously amusing that one can't help encouraging her.'

The Captivating Princess

Carrying out her first overseas engagement at the coronation of Queen Juliana of the Netherlands in September 1948, male students were so struck with the Princess's appearance and charm that they serenaded her with flowers from a canal boat on the River Amstel beneath her hotel bedroom window.

The Countess of Athlone, Princess Alice, who was related to Queen Juliana and also in Amsterdam for the ceremony, was astonished to witness the fuss surrounding the young Princess Margaret. 'She really was the centre of attention … The crowds went wild about her, shouting "Margriet! Margriet!" whenever she appeared.'

Young and Single

An American headline of the time heralded: 'She is Britain's Number One item for public scrutiny,' going on to say, 'People are more interested in her than in the House of Commons or the dollar crisis.'

The Princess was well aware of the effect her appearance had and the way in which she was described. Her biographer Tim Heald records one story that appeared in the US press around 1948:

"Look into my eyes," Princess Margaret ordered a startled dancing partner not long ago.

"I am looking into them, ma'am," he stammered.

"Well," said Margaret, "you're looking into the most beautiful eyes in England. The Duchess of Kent has the most beautiful nose. The Duchess of Windsor has the most beautiful chin. And I have the most beautiful eyes. Surely," she added, with an impish gleam in her eye, as her flustered partner groped for a suitable answer, "you believe what you read in the papers."'

Princess Margaret also joked that her intense blue eyes were, 'The only thing about me worth looking at.'

The 'Party Princess'

Time magazine in America dubbed her the 'party princess', writing, 'With sister Elizabeth safely settled in matronhood, Margaret is the most eligible party-goer in Britain … it is Princess Margaret's particular task to extend her hand to passé old Dame Society, and to make it seem that everyone is having a ripping time.'

She had gathered around herself a close circle of friends, including Sharman Douglas, the Vassar-educated daughter of the American Ambassador, and a number of wealthy young aristocrats. This lively group became known as the 'Margaret Set' and their antics were well documented in the society pages.

Margaret, however, always disputed this label. 'Most of the people who became my friends – and they generally had other and much closer friends of their own – were Sharman's friends first. So if anything, it was *her* set, not mine. There never was a "Margaret Set".'

Another American magazine, *Newsweek*, printed an anecdote about the Princess at this time. When asked to play the piano for a strict Presbyterian church minister, she had, it claimed, launched into a raucous rendition of 'I Cain't Say No' from the musical *Oklahoma!*.

The press linked the eligible young Princess's name to many possible suitors. Margaret's explanation for so many male friends was simple, 'Girls of one's own age were not really interested in what one did officially, but one's men friends were polite enough to listen.'

The Princess in Love

Group Captain Peter Townsend was an RAF officer, flying ace and war hero. He became equerry to King George VI in 1944 and met the two princesses shortly afterwards. Princess Margaret said of the dashing officer, 'My father became very fond of Peter. They both stammered and that was a bond. When he first appeared, I had a terrific crush on him. But there was no question of romance until much later – he was a married man.'

Margaret herself claimed she first fell in love with Peter Townsend when she was seventeen and he accompanied the Royal Family on their 1947 tour of South Africa. She told a friend many years later, 'We rode together every morning in that wonderful country, in marvellous weather. That's when I really fell in love with him.'

He wrote of the Princess who was then half his age: 'Throughout the daily round of civic ceremonies that pretty and highly personable young princess held her own.'

It was when he returned from the royal trip that he realised his marriage to his first wife, Rosemary Pawle, was irrevocably breaking down.

Officially, their romance began in 1952, when Margaret was twenty-two and grieving the loss of her beloved father. That was also when Peter Townsend filed for divorce on the grounds of his wife's adultery.

There's no doubt that Margaret's whole world crumbled with the death of her father. Although he had been ill for some time, his death in February 1952 came as a shock and seems to have been unexpected. The Princess spoke of this time, 'I remember feeling tunnel-visioned and didn't really notice things ... there was an awful sense of being in a black hole.'

While her sister was then completely taken up with her new responsibilities as monarch, Margaret moved out of Buckingham Palace with her grieving mother and into apartments in Clarence House.

The Palace managed to hide the relationship between the Princess and the Group Captain until the Queen's coronation in June 1953 when Margaret was seen to flick a piece of fluff from Peter Townsend's uniform outside Westminster

Abbey. The simple, but intimate gesture signalled to the press that the rumours of a romance were true. The story soon appeared in the American press, then newspapers worldwide, including Britain.

In his autobiography *Time and Chance*, written many years later when he was in his sixties, Townsend described Margaret in tender detail, 'She was a girl of unusual, intense beauty, confined as it was in her short, slender figure and centred about large purple-blue eyes, generous, sensitive lips, and a complexion as smooth as a peach. She was capable, in her face and in her whole being, of an astonishing power of expression. It could change in an instant from saintly, almost melancholic, composure to hilarious, uncontrollable joy … She could make you bend double with laughing and also touch you deeply in your heart.'

When news of the affair reached the Queen's private secretary, Sir Tommy Lascelles, he was appalled. Very much a part of the old order, he did everything in his power to put a stop to it. 'You must be either mad or bad,' Lascelles told Peter Townsend in no uncertain terms.

Until this point no one had officially told Princess Margaret or Peter Townsend that marriage was out of the question, merely that they should wait. 'Had he said we couldn't get married we wouldn't have thought any more about it. But nobody bothered to explain anything to us.'

Princess Margaret was said to blame Lascelles for ruining her life and years later when she spotted him from her car window ordered her chauffeur to 'Run the brute down!'

As Margaret was under twenty-five, she needed the Queen's consent to marry. Since Townsend was divorced, this was a problem for the Queen as head of the Church of England.

Although when first told of the relationship Prime Minister Winston Churchill had exclaimed, 'What a delightful match! A lovely young royal lady married to a gallant young airman, safe from the perils and horrors of war!' he was quickly reminded of the all too recent Abdication crisis when Margaret's uncle had given up the throne to marry a divorcee. Whilst retaining some sympathy for the Princess, Churchill agreed. The situation was too similar. Scandal must be avoided at all costs.

With the Prime Minister and Cabinet firmly set against the match, Peter Townsend was hastily dispatched to Brussels to work as air attaché for the British Embassy there. At the time, the Princess was away on a royal tour of Africa with her mother. When she heard of the move, Margaret was furious and refused to leave her room for three days. But whatever the Establishment had hoped, interest in the couple's relationship did not die down.

After two years, Margaret and Peter were reunited but the question of their marriage was still an issue. At the time, it was affirmed that if the Princess married Peter Townsend she would lose her royal privileges as well as her income. Letters that have since come to light suggest that the Prime Minister of the day, Sir Antony Eden, himself a divorcee, was trying to work out an agreement and there has been speculation that the relationship was effectively over at this point. After a fraught and tearful meeting between Margaret, her mother, her sister the Queen and Prince Philip, a formal announcement was inevitable.

Writing of those days Peter Townsend reflected, 'We were both exhausted, mentally, emotionally, physically. We felt mute and numbed at the centre of this maelstrom.

'When the Princess agreed to renounce marriage, we both had a feeling of unimaginable relief. We were liberated at last from this monstrous problem which had hung like a millstone around our necks ... At last we could talk without that crushing weight of world opinion – the sympathy, the criticism, the pity and the anger – all the mass of emotion which had weighed so heavily on our minds. There remained only the glow, once shared, of tenderness, constancy and singleness of heart.

'She could have married me only if she had been prepared to give up everything – her position, her prestige, her privy purse. I simply hadn't the weight, I knew it, to counterbalance all she would have lost. Thinking of it calmly ... you couldn't have expected her to become an ordinary housewife overnight, could you? And to be fair, I wouldn't have wanted that for her.'

Margaret later told friends that the weight of pressure from the Establishment against the relationship nearly had the opposite effect on her, 'They were so against us, it almost made me change my mind and marry him after all.'

The Princess thought she should personally inform the Archbishop of Canterbury of her decision. When she entered his office, the Archbishop Geoffrey Fisher was reaching for a book. Assuming he was about to quote something to her, Margaret said, 'You can put away your books, Archbishop. I am not going to marry Peter Townsend. I wanted you to know first.'

Duty First

Peter Townsend wrote the draft outline of the statement Princess Margaret was to make. When she read it through, she told him, 'That's exactly how I feel.'

On 31 October 1955, the Princess issued her definitive announcement to the press and public:

I would like it to be known that I have decided not to marry
Group Captain Peter Townsend. I have been aware that,
subject to my renouncing my rights of succession, it might
have been possible for me to contract a civil marriage. But
mindful of the Church's teachings that Christian marriage is
indissoluble, and conscious of my duty to the Commonwealth,
I have resolved to put these considerations before others. I
have reached this decision entirely alone, and in doing so
I have been strengthened by the unfailing support and devotion
of Group Captain Townsend. I am deeply grateful for the
concern of all those who have constantly prayed for my
happiness.

Mending a Broken Heart

Margaret was said to be heartbroken. She rarely spoke of the
affair afterwards, at least in public. However, she and Peter
Townsend remained on good terms, seeing one another for
the last time, it's believed, in 1992.

Noel Coward, who came to know the Princess fairly well,
observed in his diary: 'Townsend was a serious-minded
man who developed into a blimp, while Princess Margaret
was a vivacious, mercurial young woman anxious to sample

life in all its variety. She would have proved too much for Townsend to handle.'

The idea of the tragic Princess, who had sacrificed love for duty, became fixed in the public ideology. Margaret carried on. She claimed as always that her role was 'to help the Queen'.

Within weeks she was busier than ever, and was a regular at the theatre and concerts as well as undertaking the usual round of royal appointments.

In 1954, the Princess appeared for the first time on the New York Dress Institute's list of the world's best-dressed women. She was number eight. The Duchess of Windsor who had held the number one spot for fifteen years had dropped to tenth place.

Meanwhile, speculation grew about possible suitors for the Princess. In 1956, she was briefly and unofficially engaged to Billy Wallace. Fabulously wealthy and part of the 'Margaret Set', he had been proposing to the Princess for years. The two were friends and she accepted him at last on something of a whim, because he was 'somebody one at least liked'. Returning from a holiday in the Bahamas he confessed to a fling and a furious Princess immediately terminated the engagement. The pair remained friends, however, and Margaret was to attend both his wedding and funeral.

Towards the end of the decade, stories of the Princess's unreasonable demands became more frequent, along with rumours of her excessive drinking and smoking, her insistence on late night partying, from which no guests or staff were allowed to retire before her.

On Official Business

Princess Margaret began her royal duty as a child, making her first public broadcast alongside her sister on the BBC's *Children's Hour* radio programme in October 1940. Princess Elizabeth read a short four-minute message to 'the children of the Empire', their friends and relations, many of whom had been evacuated because of the war. At the end of the message, Elizabeth said, 'My sister is by my side and we are going to say goodnight to you. Come on, Margaret.' Ten-year-old Margaret's eager voice then rang out cheerily, 'Goodnight, children.'

As the younger sister, Margaret was very much the support act and this was to remain her role as far as official duties were concerned. She carried out her first solo public engagement at the age of twelve.

'I went to present the school prizes at the Princess Margaret School in Windsor,' the Princess remembered. When interviewed by Roy Plomley, the creator and first presenter of *Desert Island Discs* for an appearance on the BBC Radio 4 show in January 1981, she admitted that she was so nervous beforehand, she felt sick.

Her appearance on the programme was included as number 35 in a *Guardian* list of '75 defining moments from 75 years of castaways'. The Princess sounds outrageously posh and backs up this impression by choosing as two of her discs 'Rule Britannia' and also 'Scotland the Brave', about which she requested, 'I hope that it's played by the pipes and drums of my regiment, the Royal Highland Fusiliers.'

'Dear Grannie'

Biographer Tim Heald revealed that the young Princess wrote about many of her royal visits in letters to her grandmother. In May 1947, she made her first trip to Italy, telling Queen Mary: 'Travelled up from the South to Rome where we spent a week trying to see everything, which was impossible, then to Florence, also for a week and your list was a great boon and we managed to see everything you suggested. The only difficulty about seeing so many churches and picture galleries and museums on top of each other is that one can't remember what was in which place.'

Margaret may have loved Italy, but it also gave her the first real taste of the paparazzi and their frenzy for all things princess and royal. Photos were taken of her on Capri, swimming, wearing a bikini that was coyly described as 'a two-piece bathing suit'. A selection of the pictures soon appeared splashed across newspapers around the world. She quickly wrote to reassure Queen Mary, 'I do hope you didn't believe a word in any of the papers about the visit to Capri. I am afraid that they really rather overdid everything and wrote some rather vulgar and unnecessary things all of which were perfectly untrue.'

Arriving in South Africa the same year, surrounded by the full royal entourage, she was said to have commented, 'Isn't it a pity that we have to travel with royalty?'

With her elder sister married and pregnant in 1948, Princess Margaret took on more public duties, thirty-five in all that year. Arriving back from one trip, she was met at the airport by Crawfie, not long before the governess was finally allowed to retire. Crawfie reassured her that everyone was very proud of her, to which the Princess laughed and said, 'Well, I have to behave myself now, Crawfie, don't I? There is no Lilibet around, to keep me in my place with a sisterly poke.'

'I leap at the opportunity of doing lots of different things to help my sister,' Princess Margaret has said on many occasions over the years.

In spring 1949, Princess Margaret made official visits to France and Italy, where she was again mobbed by crowds and the press. '*La bella Margherita*' was the toast of the Continent, but along with the adoration came the intrusive photographs and stories. During the trip she was also granted an audience with Pope Pius XII, which created its own religious controversy about a Protestant princess meeting the Pontiff. In the event, the audience was a great success. Dressed in black, wearing a black lace mantilla, Margaret was given a crucifix by the Pope which remained a treasured possession. She recalled afterwards, 'I was so nervous I couldn't stop shaking.'

Public Life

Opening scout and guide huts also became something of a speciality. It's hard not to think her clipped speech at the official opening of the Sandringham Company Girl Guides hut is slightly tongue-in-cheek but she was only eighteen and found public speaking quite an ordeal, however confidently mature she appeared otherwise: 'Looking round me, I can imagine how hard Miss Musselwhite and the company must have worked … I do congratulate you on the charming appearance of your new meeting place. I have been in the movement ten years (doesn't that sound a long time?) as a Brownie, a Guide and now a Sea Ranger … I have now great pleasure in declaring this hut open.'

Margaret may not have had her pick of the most newsworthy royal engagements but she was a popular choice, particularly in the late 1940s and 50s when she cut a glamorous and stylish figure. Aneurin Bevan, the Labour Party Minister for Health, was always very keen for Princess Margaret to visit hospitals and pressed her office with invitations. The reason was simple. So popular was she, that every time she made a visit, recruitment numbers of nurses soared for the newly formed NHS.

After attending a Not Forgotten Association tea party in the Royal Mews in 1949, Group Captain Sir Louis Greig, an old friend of her father's and editor of the *Tatler*, wrote, 'I hope Princess Margaret was none the worse for her gloriously long stay at yesterday's party … The men were enthralled at Princess Margaret's kindness and interest and may I say it, quite glorious appearance … The singing of "She's a Jolly Good Fellow" was unexpected and entirely on the men's own. It has never been sung before on similar occasions and they all adored singing it.' He also told the Princess, 'You do give a little glamour and gaiety to a drab world.'

The Princess's one-time footman, David John Payne, was usually on-hand when the Queen Mother greeted her younger daughter on her return from official engagements. He wrote a tell-all book about his time at Clarence House, called *My Life with Princess Margaret*, which was published in 1962 in the US, though banned in the UK. In it he described one such occasion. When the Queen Mother asked Margaret, 'Did you enjoy yourself?' her daughter sighed, 'Honestly, Mother, I was bored stiff.'

Royally Rude

By nature, completely honest, Margaret's inability to temper her frankness became a flaw in the blaze of publicity.

At other times she was overheard to complain, 'All the town clerks are exactly the same …' – and after a visit to Keele University where she had just been made Chancellor she said dismissively, 'All the students at Keele have just discovered Marx.'

Although she was once banned from the annual ball there and a motion put forward for her replacement, she was surprisingly successful in her role. She was Keele University's longest serving Chancellor, from 1962 to 1986, and had been President of its forerunner, the University College of North Staffordshire. Viewing a sculpture by Jacob Epstein there in 1961, one committee member broke all the protocol rules they had previously been given by asking directly, 'What do you think your sister will make of it?' Margaret is said to have chuckled.

At a dinner to mark the opening of the new Students' Union building in early 1963, all elements of the menu had been carefully agreed in advance with Clarence House. However, when the catering manager brought in the huge unmoulded crème caramel he had made for dessert, Princess Margaret remarked aloud, 'I don't eat crème caramel.'

Meeting one official who explained rather pompously, 'I'm in textiles and I sit on the Bench', the Princess was withering in her response. 'You sit on the bench in textiles,' she paused. 'How interesting, but uncomfortable.'

The Princess was not known to put on a performance to please the public and could be brusque in her approach. A member of one women's organisation commented, 'I'm afraid we weren't very impressed. We had all worked so hard and looked forward to her visit so much. But she just didn't seem interested. You felt that she was just getting through the whole business as quickly as she could. She only spoke to a couple of officials and that was that.'

Another was more forthright, 'I was furious. When I meet a princess, I expect her to behave like a princess. It's the least she can do.'

Offerings of food often provoked the Princess's scorn. Writer and photographer Christopher Simon Sykes recalled a visit Margaret had made to his diplomat father's home. Staff had prepared a lavish afternoon tea. The Princess took one look and announced, 'I hate tea!'

On another occasion, journalist and broadcaster Matthew Parris remembered her opening some offices and sheltered homes for the elderly in the Derbyshire constituency where he was then Tory MP. As a nod to royalty, coronation chicken had been specially cooked for the Princess. 'This looks like sick,' was her only comment.

On an official trip to Germany in 1980, when she was due to review an army regiment that had been especially lined up to receive the royal visitor, Princess Margaret refused to leave her car because she 'felt too cold'.

When questioned about her bored or disapproving look at official engagements, Princess Margaret claimed it was, 'A defence mechanism. I'm not aware that I am doing it.'

She could be contradictory. Asked whether some of her public work was boring, Margaret was diplomatic in her reply, 'No. Some of the things one does can be, but I've got a reflex against it now. I think it's very much up to one not to be bored.'

After an official lunch, when the chairman of a police committee asked her, 'How shall I introduce you – "Your Royal Highness" or what?' he earned himself one of the Princess's epic putdowns.

'Does it really matter?' she asked, at her most withering. 'You've been calling me "love" for the last two hours.'

At other times the Princess appeared completely at ease and in her element. The glass of whisky and cigarette may have made her look an unlikely President of the Girl Guide Association, but she had loved her own time as a Guide and was enthusiastic in her role. 'It soon became obvious that she knew as much about the Association as any of the well-scrubbed ladies in navy suits and badges,' observed a fellow attendee of a Guiding reception.

An ardent ballet fan, Princess Margaret relished her role as President of the Royal Ballet. She enjoyed meeting the dancers backstage 'whatever you are wearing' and was friendly and relaxed in their company, joining in the chat and gossip. 'She's a very nice woman,' was the usual verdict afterwards.

Changing Times

By the late 1950s, the presentation of debutantes at court as part of their 'coming out' London Season appeared increasingly out of touch with a more modern Britain. The Queen ended the practice in 1958 and instead began inviting a wider cross section of guests to garden parties at Buckingham Palace and Holyroodhouse.

This change in royal tradition was met with waspish relief by Princess Margaret, who commented sardonically, 'We had to end it. Every tart in London was getting in.'

Politics and the Princess

On the topic of politicians, Margaret was characteristically blunt: 'I hate them. They never listen to anything I say or answer my questions. Even Sir Winston Churchill would just grunt.'

As with Prince Philip in his early years as Queen's consort, Margaret had no defined role to fulfil, and both were very much sidelined. Prince Philip remained bitter that the Establishment and politicians, Churchill chief amongst them, had insisted his children could not keep his surname, and Princess Margaret had much to complain about in the official handling of her affair with Peter Townsend, not least the manner in which he was instantly dispatched to Brussels without even being allowed to see her to say goodbye.

Although obviously not a fan of politicians, the Princess seems to have made an exception for Margaret Thatcher. The Prime Minister had written to her while Margaret was staying at the London Clinic for a minor operation in early 1980. The Princess's handwritten reply covered various surprising topics:

I find it quite impossible to find out what is happening in Afghanistan. Are they about to wheel into Iran and get all the oil? More power to your policy of nuclear power stations. I wish they weren't called 'nuclear' as people always think of the bomb. I've been advocating this since I was twenty!

I was so interested to hear about your visit to the United States. I expect you surprised them no end at answering their questions in a positive way, when they are used to waffling for hours in figures of eight, not actually answering anything.

I went to Cambridge for a debate (rather dull, all about the church, lots of clerics) and found them all rabid conservatives – not a Trotskyite to argue with!

More predictably she thanked the Prime Minister for her donation to the NSPCC (National Society for the Prevention of Cruelty to Children): 'They are vital and I am President and support their free service.'

The Charitable Princess

The work of the NSPCC was always close to Margaret's heart. Appointed President at the age of twenty-three, the Princess made a lifelong commitment to the organisation. After a visit by Princess Margaret to Northern Ireland in 1996 on behalf of the charity, the president of the County Armagh branch, Bertie Shields, said: 'It was a real boost to morale to have her here. She was really lovely.'

Patricia McGoldrick of the Shankill centre said, 'She is very in touch with our work. The Princess told me how someone had once described child abuse as normal because there seems to be so much publicity and how she immediately took a step back and said: "How can child abuse ever be normal?"'

'As a public figure, she showed her support for a cause which is still unpopular today,' David Wakefield of the Terrence Higgins Trust (a British charity that campaigns on and provides services relating to HIV and sexual health) said, after the Princess's death. Margaret became patron of the Trust in 2000. Her long-standing friend and lady-in-waiting Anne Tennant explained that they used to go there regularly, long before the publicity of Princess Diana's visits.

During an average year, Princess Margaret carried out in the region of 150 official engagements, including opening ceremonies, charity appearances, investitures, dinners and receptions. She also travelled extensively abroad on state visits and was patron or president of over fifty different societies and trusts.

On learning that her sister was about to make a royal visit to Morocco, the Princess had this piece of advice to offer, 'Going to Morocco, you'll find, is rather like being kidnapped; you never know where you are going or with whom.'

On one occasion, after refusing a journalist's request for an interview, Princess Margaret passed on a message through her friend Lady Prue Penn, to explain, 'Tell her that everything I do is to support the Queen and to help her.'

Countess Snowdon

Princess Margaret first met Antony Armstrong-Jones at a Chelsea dinner party in May 1958. They were guests of one of the Princess's ladies-in-waiting, Lady Elizabeth Cavendish. Tall and aristocratic, Lady Elizabeth was the sister of the Duke of Devonshire and long-time lover and companion of the poet Sir John Betjeman. Her Chelsea townhouse on Cheyne Walk provided the perfect setting for an eclectic mix of artists, bohemian intellectuals and aristocrats. Amongst them, Princess Margaret found photographer Tony Armstrong-Jones refreshingly different. He was animated and daring, unfazed by her position, but suitably charming. He was just five months older than her, slightly built and like her, short.

A Different World

From her own account, Princess Margaret didn't take the photographer's attentions too seriously at first. She told her biographer Christopher Warwick, 'I enjoyed his company very much, but I didn't take a lot of notice of him because I thought he was queer.'

In fact, Tony Armstrong-Jones himself commented on his rumoured bisexuality, 'I didn't fall in love with boys, but a few men have been in love with me.'

He and the Princess began to spend an increasing amount of time with one another, but their developing relationship was a well-kept secret.

'What is a bohemian? What does it mean?' Margaret asked her lady-in-waiting, Elizabeth Cavendish, in reference to Tony.

Lady Cavendish replied, 'Well, ma'am, it means he won't always turn up to lunch when he says he will.'

As a mark of their growing closeness, Antony Armstrong-Jones was invited to take the official photographs of Princess Margaret to celebrate her twenty-ninth birthday. When she bumped into the usual royal photographer, Cecil Beaton, she joked, 'I've been faithless to you.'

Beaton noted in his diary, 'I knew at once that she meant that she had had her photograph taken by TAJ. This was a blow, but I thought it extremely honest and frank to tell me before the pictures appeared. I showed great tact by muttering, "I'm so glad. He's such a nice young man and deserves his success."'

At the time, Beaton did not suspect there was anything other than a purely professional relationship between TAJ and HRH.

Later, the Princess was to say that Antony Armstrong-Jones made her feel 'daring'. She added, 'He understood my job and pushed me to do things. In a way he introduced me to a new world.'

That new world included his hideaway in Rotherhithe, a small, terraced house backing on to the river Thames surrounded by south-east London warehouses, where Armstrong-Jones rented a room.

Margaret remembered the place fondly: 'It had the most marvellous view. One walked into the room and there was the river straight in front. At high tide, swans looked in. And because it was on the bend of the river, you looked towards the Tower and Tower Bridge with the dome of St Paul's behind them, to the left and the docks to the right.'

She called it, 'The little white roomo.'

Princess Margaret might have enjoyed the novel simplicity of the Docklands house where Tony's actor and artist friends would drop by for casual drinks and supper, but others of the photographer's old circle remembered the evenings rather differently. Actor Tony Richardson wrote in his autobiography *A Long Distance Runner*: 'These evenings were rather stilted and stiff … she wasn't at ease at the time, and nor was anyone else much. There were awkward questions of protocol – no one was supposed to leave before the Princess, which, as I was rehearsing early, was impossible for me … I didn't enjoy them and soon stopped attending.'

Tony Armstrong-Jones may have followed stricter royal protocol at first – showing the Princess just enough deference alongside the daring – but he soon dropped the 'ma'am'. In private, he called her 'M', 'Pet' and sometimes 'Ducky', while she referred to him as 'Tone'.

Royal Engagement

When the Queen Mother announced the engagement of her 'beloved daughter The Princess Margaret Rose to Mr Antony Armstrong-Jones' on 26 February 1960, the news surprised almost everyone, including the press. A fact that pleased the couple who had been zipping around the London streets for months, with the Princess incognito on the back of Tony's motorbike.

The pair became privately engaged after Tony proposed.

'He eventually did, but in a roundabout way. It was very cleverly worded,' Margaret said enigmatically.

Though it is not known whether the ring really was hidden inside a number of boxes as depicted in the popular TV series *The Crown*, Margaret's future husband did present her with a ruby ring that he'd had designed to look like a rosebud.

Armstrong-Jones's proposal came shortly after Peter Townsend had written to Margaret telling her that he was about to announce his engagement to a young Belgian woman, Marie-Luce Jamagne. The Princess always denied that she had accepted Tony on the rebound, but there's no doubt she felt betrayed by Townsend as they had made a pact not to marry.

The speed of the proposal was evident, however. When the Queen Mother expressed her delight at the news that Armstrong-Jones was to marry Margaret in December 1959, he said, 'Ssh! I haven't asked the Queen yet!'

Queen Elizabeth II gave her formal consent to the marriage in January 1960, but as she was then pregnant, royal protocol meant that she asked her sister to delay making the announcement until after the birth of Prince Andrew on 19 February 1960.

Tony's professional rival, Cecil Beaton, was furious at the news, ranting that the younger Armstrong-Jones was, 'Not even a good photographer!' Though to the Princess he offered his gracious congratulations and added, 'May I thank you, ma'am, for removing my most dangerous rival.'

Always quick-witted and ready with a snappy riposte, Margaret enjoyed teasing people. She delightedly answered back, 'What makes you think Tony is going to give up work?'

The groom's father had misgivings about the match. Barrister Ronald Armstrong-Jones said, 'I wish in heaven's name this hadn't happened. It will never work out. Tony's a far too independent sort of fellow to be subjected to discipline. He won't be prepared to play second fiddle to anyone. He will have to walk two steps behind his wife, and I fear for his future.'

It should be noted that Armstrong-Jones senior had just married his third wife.

Novelist Kingsley Amis was bluntly colourful in his views on the engagement. He had previously met Armstrong-Jones and had happened to criticise the Princess saying amongst other things, 'the woman obviously has no mind at all.'

The photographer had corrected him, 'I can assure you you're quite wrong, she is in fact an extremely intelligent and well-informed woman,' though admitting only that he had 'met her on several occasions.'

Now Amis let rip in a letter to a friend: 'Such a symbol of the age we live in, when a royal princess, famed for her devotion to all that is most vapid and mindless in the world of entertainment, her habit of reminding people of her status whenever they venture to disagree with her in conversation and appalling taste in clothes, is united with a dog-faced tight-jeaned fotog of fruitarian tastes such as can be found in dozens in any pseudo-arty drinking cellar in fashionable-unfashionable London. They're made for each other.'

The Queen held a party to celebrate the match on 4 May 1960. An intimate occasion for 2,000 guests at Buckingham Palace, where Joe Loss rather appropriately played songs from the musical *Fings Ain't What They Used to Be*, 'and Armstrong-Jones's bohemian friends mingled with staid members of the Establishment.'

Princess Bride

The wedding took place at Westminster Abbey on 6 May 1960. It marked a new era as the first royal wedding to be televised and was watched by a staggering 300 million viewers around the world. Prince Philip stood in to give the bride away and she wore a dress by Norman Hartnell. *Life* magazine described it as 'the simplest royal wedding gown in history'. This was down to the groom's input. He reportedly gave the designer his own sketch for the dress and insisted on no 'glitter' or adornment.

On the subject of televising the ceremony, the Princess said, 'It meant that those of my friends who couldn't come could still see it. I loved that idea.'

Walking his sister-in-law along the aisle towards her waiting groom, Prince Philip asked, 'Am I holding on to you, or are you holding on to me?'

'I'm holding on to you,' Margaret whispered back.

'I don't know who's more nervous, you or me,' Philip replied.

Even royalty get wedding jitters and fluff their lines. During the ceremony, repeating her marriage vows after the Archbishop of Canterbury, Margaret missed a line, 'I knew the words so well. I'd practised them over and over, so that instead of repeating "From this day forward" I beat the Archbishop to the next line, "For better, for worse".'

Noel Coward described the day in his diary:

'The morning was brilliant and the crowds lining the streets looked like endless vivid herbaceous borders. The police were smiling, the Guards beaming and the air tingling with excitement and the magic of spring ... [the bride] looked like the ideal of what any fairy-tale princess should look like. Tony Armstrong-Jones pale, and a bit tremulous and completely charming ... it was lusty, charming, romantic, splendid and without a false note. It is still a pretty exciting thing to be English.'

After the ceremony, came the ride back to Buckingham Palace in the Glass Coach, the wedding breakfast and then the couple departed for a six-week honeymoon on board the royal yacht *Britannia*, bound for the Caribbean.

Married Life

Returning from their honeymoon, the couple moved into an apartment at 10 Kensington Palace, its redesign closely monitored by Tony.

Disgruntled, the Princess complained that her ten-bedroom marital home was so cramped it was 'like a doll's house'. They still kept the room in Rotherhithe where they would escape on Tony's motorbike.

Nicky Haslam, the interior designer and socialite, who first met Princess Margaret when they were children, said after she died, 'I think Margaret was at her happiest during her early years with Snowdon. She looked wonderful and they were so good together. They were a wonderful double act; they played off each other and had a charming rivalry. There was always humour and fun with them.'

Noel Coward wrote after an evening that had taken in both Kensington Palace and Rotherhithe, 'They were both very sweet and obviously very happy.'

> Magazine publisher Jocelyn Stevens was one of Tony's oldest friends and also knew the Princess well. He commented, 'I have always regarded her as a bird in a gilded cage. She would have loved to break free, but was never able to.' For a while, it seemed as though Armstrong-Jones offered her this freedom.

In October 1961, Tony finally accepted the earldom he had been offered and became the first Earl of Snowdon, Viscount

Linley of Nymans – more usually known as Lord Snowdon. For a while, he and Margaret appeared the perfect modern couple, a fixture on the sixties London social scene, arty and glamorously attractive.

At the start of their married life, Tony gave up his career to act as Margaret's consort, but it was clear early on this was not going to work.

'It was like a pilot sacrificing his career for his marriage … but watching every plane with the thought, "I should be up there,"' Jocelyn Stevens said.

Tony joined the Council of Industrial Design as an advisor and during this time, worked on a new aviary for London Zoo. He gradually took on more photographic assignments and at the start of 1962 was offered the post of artistic advisor to *The Sunday Times*.

Family Life

Lord Snowdon and Princess Margaret's son, David Albert Charles, was born on 3 November 1961 and given the title Viscount Linley.

'The Princess and I are absolutely thrilled and delighted,' Lord Snowdon said at the time.

On 1 May 1964, their daughter, Sarah Frances Elizabeth, was born at their new, larger apartment at 1A Kensington Palace. The family had moved in the previous year.

In August 1964, the Snowdons went away on holiday with Jocelyn Stevens and his family. Stevens wrote enthusiastically afterwards, 'I called Princess Margaret "the Master Planner". She loved planning what we were going to do and keeps the most marvellous albums which she faithfully writes up … She loved it. It was the most marvellous holiday and she and Tony got on so well.'

In a comment recognising the tediousness of museum or gallery visits as a child, Margaret attempted to make such outings more interesting, 'When I grew up I decided my children should never be allowed to see more than three great pictures at a time, so that they would actually plead for "just one more", instead of dropping with fatigue.'

She also instilled some royal life-lessons in David and Sarah: 'We were taught to go on – with the flu, fever, whatever. One of the things I taught my children is, whenever you say you're going some place, never chuck it. And especially, never chuck one invitation for a better one.'

As someone with a keen interest in history, Princess Margaret recalled, 'I used to tell my children to remember, in their old age, that when they were young they had known someone who had known someone who had danced at a ball just before the Battle of Waterloo.' She was referring to their relative, Princess Alice, Countess of Athlone, who told the story of how she knew a woman who had been a guest at the Duchess of Richmond's ball in Brussels on the eve of the Battle in 1815.

The Party's Over

When asked why she had married Antony Armstrong-Jones after the couple's divorce in 1978, Margaret answered, 'I didn't really want to marry at all. Why did I? Because he asked me! Really, though, he was such a nice person in those days.'

One of her husband's friends explained it rather more basically as: 'Sex, sex, sex. Theirs was a terribly physical relationship. They couldn't keep their hands off each other, even with other people present.'

Journalist and expert on etiquette, Drusilla Beyfus knew the Snowdons well and thought the writing was on the wall for their relationship quite early on, 'She and Tony were a glamorous couple. But there was a halo of anxiety about the way things would go. Because quite soon it was apparent they weren't getting on.'

The Princess's cousin, Margaret Rhodes, observed simply, 'Tony and she were both very determined and highly individual.'

Even Tony's close friends admitted that he could be cruel. Restless by nature, photographic assignments gave him the perfect excuse to travel alone. The more absent he was, the more possessive and insecure Princess Margaret became.

He persuaded his wife that she really needed to see a psychiatrist and she duly visited Dr Peter Dally in 1966. Afterwards she said, 'Tony sent me to him. He said it would be the answer. But I only lasted one session – I didn't like it at all. Perfectly useless!'

> Tony would play on his wife's insecurities, tricking her into wearing a ball gown when everyone else was casually dressed, needling her into throwing a tantrum in front of the Royal family or immediately before a public event. He left notes saying, 'I hate you' tucked into her books and once wrote a list for her to find entitled 'Twenty-four reasons why I hate you'.
>
> Justifiably upset, Margaret said to a friend, 'I can't think of twenty-four reasons to hate anybody.'

A constant source of friction was the Princess's insistence upon staying up late, drinking, playing the piano or partying.

She seldom went to bed before midnight and no one else, including her husband, was allowed to retire ahead of her.

Lord Snowdon wasn't the only one with marital gripes it seems. When Margaret attended a high-society party in New York, the hostess asked politely how was the Queen?

'Which one?' Margaret replied coolly. 'My sister, my mother, or my husband?'

Marital Discord

Neither were faithful. If Princess Margaret hoped to make her husband jealous by having a brief fling with his old Eton schoolmate Antony Barton, she did not succeed. The two friends were quickly reconciled, although Barton's wife never really forgave Margaret.

In 1967, the Princess began seeing Robin Douglas-Home, a pianist and nephew of the former Conservative Prime Minister, Alec Douglas-Home. Finding out about their relationship, Tony persuaded Margaret to end the affair. Her letters doing so came to light many years later:

I am hampered by thoughts and hearts being divided at this moment when a real effort must be made on my side to make the marriage work. I feel I can do this, curiously enough, more convincingly with this happiness of security in you, and feeling of being upheld by you, than without … Trust me as I trust you … Our love has the passionate scent of new-mown grass and lilies about it … Promise me that you will never give up, that you will go on encouraging me to make the marriage a success, and that given a good and safe chance, I will try and come back to you one day.

The story has a sad ending. Unsuccessful as a musician, sacked by his latest employer and desperately short of money, Douglas-Home committed suicide eighteen months after the end of the affair.

With Snowdon again away travelling for work in early 1967, the press began to get wind of rifts in the marriage. The rumours reached such a level that Tony felt compelled to issue a formal statement denying difficulties:

Nothing has happened to our marriage. When I am away – and I'm away quite a lot on assignments for my paper – I write home and I telephone like other husbands in love with their wives. I telephoned today. I can't understand what started this, but some of these papers have been hinting about this since six months after my marriage. No responsible journalist could possibly take seriously such silly stories.

Princess Margaret remembered things a little differently: 'He never rang or wrote when he was abroad, which made it awkward when friends asked for news of him.'

By the early 1970s, Princess Margaret had taken to talking freely to journalist and gossip columnist Nigel Dempster. She would often tell him unflattering stories about people she disliked or those who had fallen from favour, which would then appear in the press attributed to 'a source close to the Palace' or 'a close friend'. As the Snowdons' marriage unravelled, Princess Margaret began to speak remarkably openly about her relationship with her husband.

Discussing Tony's ongoing relationship with Lucy Lindsay-Hogg (who he went on to marry in 1978), Margaret said: 'There he was, living in my house, thinking he could have a lovely affair. I asked him for a separation but he laughed in my face. I would only know he was back at night when I heard him banging about in the bathroom – it was all hours. And he was drinking a lot of vodka in the morning, a bottle of wine at lunch and he even used to take a bottle up to his room afterwards. He was like an alcoholic. He was becoming a virtual stranger and we would meet on the stairs and growl at each other. And I had to go on behaving as if nothing was happening.'

In 1973, Princess Margaret met Roddy Llewellyn at a house party in Scotland hosted by Colin Tennant. They began the seven-year affair that was to change the public's perception of the Princess forever. The young landscape gardener was seventeen years her junior, a fact the press loved to emphasise.

Royal Divorce

After photographs taken on Mustique of Margaret and Roddy Llewellyn were leaked to the press in February 1976, lurid headlines followed about the ageing, jet-setting Princess and her toy-boy lover. Tony was able to present himself as the injured, humiliated party. Margaret told journalist Nigel Dempster some years later that, 'Lord Snowdon was devilish cunning.'

Still on holiday in Mustique, Princess Margaret heard the news that her husband was leaving from her press secretary, Lord Nigel Napier. Not trusting the phone lines to be private, he tried to deliver the news in a slightly cryptic fashion, using Snowdon's middle name: 'Ma'am, I have been talking to Robert. He has given in his notice. He will be leaving by the end of the week.'

Once she finally realised what was being said, the Princess was delighted, 'Oh, I see! Thank you, Nigel. I think that's the best news you've ever given me.'

When news of the couple's separation broke, Snowdon was away working on assignment in Sydney, Australia. On seeing footage of her estranged husband looking suitably miserable, Princess Margaret commented drily, 'I have never seen such good acting.'

After two years of separation, the official announcement of their decision to divorce came on 10 May 1978. The irony was not lost on the Princess, that having been forced to give up the man she had originally wanted to marry precisely because he was divorced, she then became the first royal to divorce since Queen Victoria's granddaughter, Princess Victoria Melita, in 1901.

However vitriolic and cruel the couple were to each other when married, after their divorce they remained on good terms, as the Princess had with all her exes.

The Glitterati: Famous Friends

When it came to famous friends, Princess Margaret got off to an early start. Author and creator of Peter Pan, James M. Barrie had sat beside the Princess at her third birthday party at Glamis Castle. He told the story, 'Some of her presents were on the table, simple things that might have come from the sixpenny shops but she was in a frenzy of glee over them, especially about one to which she had given the place of honour by her plate. I said to her as one astounded, "Is that really your very own?" and she saw how I envied her and immediately placed it between us with the words, "It is yours and mine."'

Sometime later, when Barrie's name was mentioned, the little Princess said, 'I know that man. He is my greatest friend, and I am his greatest friend.'

The lines struck a chord with Barrie, who used both in his 1936 play, *The Boy David*. He promised Margaret he would pay her a royalty of a penny each time they were spoken on stage. A solemn agreement to the deal was drawn up between the writer and the Princess.

Long before any acrimony in their marriage set in, Princess Margaret and Lord Snowden were regarded as a glamorous young couple and held regular soirees at their Kensington Palace apartment. Margaret often played the piano and liked to sing songs from popular musicals of the day. Noel Coward was a frequent guest and remarked on how 'charming' these events were. Although he could be viciously honest in his opinions, Coward wrote in his diary, 'Princess Margaret is surprisingly good. She has an impeccable ear, her piano playing is simple but has perfect rhythm, and her method of singing is really very funny.'

However, comments about her were not always so positive and she may have come to see the sense in her great great grandmother Queen Victoria's warning: 'Beware of artists, they mix with all classes of society and are therefore most dangerous.'

Society photographer Cecil Beaton had a somewhat mixed view of the Princess. At a sitting when she was in her very early twenties he wrote in his diary that it had been hard work as Margaret 'had been out at a nightclub until five-thirty the morning before and got a bit tired after two hours' posing.' Nevertheless, he conceded, 'She is witty and seems quite kindly disposed towards humanity.'

Princess Margaret confided to close friends that as the society photographer could be so waspish in company she felt obliged to invite him to dine with her alone. These private suppers seemed to work in persuading Beaton that he was particularly special to the Princess.

'One Hip Chick'

Princess Margaret enjoyed socialising and mixed with many of the most well-known figures of her time. Several also had their own private nicknames for Margaret. Trumpeter Louis Armstrong described her as 'one hip chick', while John Lennon called her 'Priceless Margarine' and her husband 'Bony Armstrove'. The comedian John Fortune referred to her as 'the pocket battleship' – a comment on both her height and character.

Princess Margaret was first introduced to The Beatles in November 1963 after they appeared for the only time at a Royal Variety Performance. She met them again with Lord Snowdon after the July 1964 premiere of their film, *A Hard Day's Night*.

The Princess was an enthusiastic fan: 'I adored them because they were poets as well as musicians.'

John Lennon's first wife, Cynthia, claimed the admiration was mutual: 'When it came to meeting royalty in the flesh, John was as much in awe as the rest of us. He was so pleased and proud that the Princess had come to see the film that his anti-Establishment views flew out of the window and he stood red-faced as she spoke to him.'

Perhaps as a result, Margaret was willing to overlook some breaks with the usual Royal rules. At the film's after party, the Princess and her husband were clearly enjoying themselves but protocol dictated that no one could eat until HRH had left. George Harrison was hungry and, getting to a point where he could wait no longer, he approached Princess Margaret and said, 'Your Highness, we really are hungry and we can't eat until you two go.'

Margaret merely nodded and replied, 'I see. Well, in that case, we'd better run.'

A year later, the Snowdons delayed their summer holiday to go along to the premiere of The Beatles' second film, *Help!*

At a Chelsea party held by the artist Rory McEwen, George Harrison arrived late having just been bailed after an arrest for possession of cannabis. He hurried up to the Princess and explained, 'We've been busted. [The police] planted hash in my bedroom closet.' Margaret was suitably sympathetic, but George was hoping she might use her influence to get the charges dropped.

The Princess was diplomatic but firm in her response, 'I don't really think so. It could become a little sticky. Sorry, George.'

George Harrison's sister-in-law, Paula Boyd, then produced a joint from her handbag and proceeded to offer it to the Princess. 'Here, do you want this?' At which point the Snowdons left.

A popular anecdote from the 1960s tells how Princess Margaret was seated next to the supermodel Twiggy at a London dinner party. Having ignored the model for much of the meal, she finally turned to her to ask, 'And who are you?'

Twiggy answered, 'Lesley Hornby, ma'am, but people call me Twiggy.'

'How unfortunate,' came the caustic response, as the Princess turned away again.

When the Princess met the performers backstage after the 1968 Royal Variety Performance, a member of the Supremes, Mary Wilson, was somewhat taken aback when Margaret asked her bluntly, 'Is that a wig you're wearing, Mary?'

Not the sort of polite royal chitchat she was expecting.

The actor and comedian Peter Sellers and his second wife, actress Britt Ekland, became good friends with the Snowdons, frequently visiting them at their home in Kensington Palace.

On one such occasion it was suggested that Tony should photograph Britt.

'He's actually quite good, Britt, if he remembers to put film in the camera,' was Princess Margaret's typically backhanded compliment.

The four went on to shoot a home movie together – the £6,000 it cost paid for by Sellers – as a thirty-ninth birthday present for the Queen in 1964. In the film, entitled *I Say I Say I Say*, the actor announces he is about to give his 'celebrated impression of Her Royal Highness Princess Margaret'. Peter Sellers then steps behind a screen, apparently executing a quick change of costume, before the real Princess Margaret steps out and takes a bow.

Another scene shows Lord Snowdon and Peter Sellers as American mobsters discussing how to murder a fellow gangster and ends with Sellers calling Snowdon a 'camp cow' to the strains of 'Love is the Sweetest Thing'. The finale has the cast, including Sellers and the Princess, performing a raucous rendition of the song 'We're Riding Along On the Crest of a Wave.'

When Peter Sellers screened the film to a party of friends, many of whom were fellow actors, the Princess exclaimed, 'I do feel such a fool. Me, an amateur, being watched by all you professionals.'

The film, however, proved a hit with the Queen and Royal Family, especially Prince Charles, who was always a huge fan of the Goon Show and Peter Sellers.

One evening at a Mayfair restaurant in London, Peter Sellers was dining with Princess Margaret, Lord Snowdon and the film director Bryan Forbes and his actress wife Nanette Newman.

At another table were songwriter Leslie Bricusse and his wife, the actor Laurence Harvey with his girlfriend, model Paulene Stone, and the actor and comedian Dudley Moore.

'He had perfected the super-slurred drunken voice that he was later to use to Oscar-nominated acclaim in the film *Arthur*, and he was on a deadly Dudley roll that had us convulsed with laughter throughout the meal,' Leslie Bricusse remembered of Moore.

At the end of dinner they went across to the Princess's table. 'Dudley, drunk with success at his surefire humour, was on a high. He just wouldn't give up. He lurched over to their table, playing it drunker than ever, gave Princess Margaret a sweeping courtly bow and slurred, "G'd evenin', your Royal Highness ... I s'pose a blow-job is out of the question?"'

By the end of the 1960s, Sellers' marriage to Ekland was over and he was declaring himself in love with Princess Margaret. He claimed to friends that they were having an affair whilst protesting to the *Daily Mirror* they were 'just good friends', knowing exactly how the statement would be interpreted. He seemed to hope they might even marry one day. Sellers was obsessed and occasionally went too far, for instance when he telephoned Margaret pretending to be Lord Snowdon describing the most intimate details of his affair with Lady Jacqueline Rufus Isaacs.

The Princess once admitted that Sellers was 'the most difficult man I know'.

> When pressed on whether Margaret had ever
> slept with the actor, a close member of staff said,
> 'Well, if she did, she had her eyes closed and
> she forgot about it immediately afterwards.'

Finally, Sellers accepted their relationship wasn't going anywhere: 'Princess Margaret has made it quite clear she won't marry again. Having been through it once and, God knows, marriage breakdowns happen all the time, she won't do it again. She is a very resolute woman.'

The Princess had also, by 1973, met Roddy Llewellyn.

Over the years there was a growing list of people with whom Princess Margaret was said to have had sexual relations. The suggestions range from the more predictable to the frankly surprising and include: Mick Jagger, Warren Beatty, Danny Kaye, Eddie Fisher, David Niven, Peter O'Toole, Sharman Douglas, Dusty Springfield, Lord Patrick Lichfield, John Spencer-Churchill, Prince Philip and John Turner, the Canadian Prime Minister.

Theatre critic Kenneth Tynan, not the easiest person to impress, defended his friendship with Princess Margaret, claiming that he liked her because of her 'appetite for the theatre, her wit and her loyalty to her friends'.

The effect of meeting the Princess could be quite overwhelming, even for the most famous. Actor Marlon Brando found himself completely tongue-tied at a dinner with Princess Margaret and Kenneth Tynan in Beauchamp Place, Knightsbridge.

The day afterwards, the Princess told Tynan that this happened quite often, explaining, 'People just clam up. I'm told it's like going on television for the first time.'

Writer and satirist John Fortune described meeting her at the BBC in the early seventies. Quickly running out of conversation, he made his excuses to leave, whereupon the Princess pulled rank: 'She fixed me with a beady look,' Fortune recalled. 'No, you don't,' she said. 'No one leaves my presence until I give them permission to do so.' He added that he thought he could see 'a look of mischief in her eyes', that he was being tested and there would have been no repercussions should he choose to go anyway. However, he did not quite dare take the risk and stayed on.

Gore Vidal first met Princess Margaret in Rome in 1965, and they went on to become good friends. He described his first impressions: 'The Princess arrived with her husband and turned out to be quite splendid, droll, with at least three manners, all beguiling. One: gracious lady visiting the troops. Two: bitchy young matron with a cold eye for contemporaries. Three: a splendid Edith Evans delivery (Q. Victoria with slow measured accents): "We are not partial to heights" she intoned gravely over a chicken wing, "not partial at all." That took care of Switzerland.'

He later also remarked, 'Like so many good-looking women, Princess Margaret likes plain-looking women ...'

Vidal often experienced the quarrelling Snowdons first hand. He described them as 'both nice separately but together hell.'

The Princess visited Vidal's house in Hollywood and he claimed, 'Like many British royals, she was fascinated by the place.' In a photograph taken there in 1978 she stands between actor Jack Nicholson and film director Tony Richardson, while Vidal appears to be whispering in her ear. He also visited Royal Lodge in Windsor in 1983, which Margaret helpfully described for him: 'You can easily recognise it. It is very pink.'

It was at Royal Lodge that Vidal was also introduced to the Queen, and Margaret once asserted, 'The trouble with Gore is that he wants my sister's job.'

> The Princess paid a typically ambiguous
> compliment to Gore Vidal's 1983 novel
> *Duluth* – which he considered one of his best
> works: 'I don't know what there is in me that
> is so low and base that I love this book.'

At a literary lunch at The Ivy in London in 1995, Vidal was in sparkling form, regaling his companions with memories including: 'For as my dear friend Princess Margaret once remarked to me in a moment of unusual candour: "Gore, you are positively the cleverest, funniest and best-read man I have ever been lucky enough to meet!"

'And do you know what I replied? I believe it is in all the standard books of my quotations, but it remains – as dear Jackie O used to say whenever I opened my mouth – always worth repeating. I replied: "You are astonishingly youthful, ma'am – and most gracious and amusing with it!"'

A Royal Obsession

There was something about the persona of Princess Margaret that sent normally sane men a little crazy. In his book *Ma'am Darling*, Craig Brown writes that artist Pablo Picasso had erotic dreams about her, admitting to his friend Roland Penrose: 'If they knew what I had done in my dreams with your royal ladies, they would take me to the Tower of London and chop off my head!' Picasso would sometimes include the Queen, too. When he bought Villa La Californie at Cannes in 1955, the young Princess Margaret seemed to him the perfect bride to be its chatelaine. She remained blissfully unaware, but he continued to harbour hopes that they might be married for years.

Author John Fowles noted in his diary in March 1951, 'I have day-dreamed of seducing Princess Margaret.' More disturbingly, he admitted that his creepy novel *The Collector* had at its core his own 'lifelong fantasy of imprisoning a girl … it used often to be famous people, Princess Margaret, various film stars …'

By comparison and rather more innocent, was the interest of various well known-poets. Among them, Philip Larkin watched the Princess from afar, writing in the 1980s, 'Nice photo of Princess Margaret in the S. Times this week wearing a Lo Lollo Waspie …' and that he had been 'meditating a poem on Princess Margaret, having to knock off first the booze and now the fags – now that's the kind of royal poem I could write with feeling.'

Sir John Betjeman was quite overwhelmed by the Princess when he first met her and later came to refer to her as 'little friend'. She would often accompany her lady-in-waiting Lady Elizabeth Cavendish, Betjeman's long-term companion, as she pushed the poet in his wheelchair from her Cheyne Walk house in Chelsea to church.

Hollywood

As Gore Vidal observed, Margaret was famously dismissive of other beautiful women, including Hollywood actresses.

Meeting Grace Kelly, who was then Princess Grace of Monaco, Princess Margaret said coolly, 'You don't look like a movie star.'

More than a little offended, Grace Kelly is said to have replied, 'Well, I wasn't born a movie star.'

Whenever she repeated this story, Princess Grace would flush with embarrassment.

Margaret was not overly impressed by Elizabeth Taylor, either. In the early 1980s, when the actress was appearing in the play *Little Foxes* at the Victoria Palace Theatre, she joined a dinner party at the Princess's home at Kensington Palace. Lord Snowdon's old friend Jeremy Fry noticed the famous actress's arrival and alerted the Princess, 'Oh, ma'am, Elizabeth Taylor has just arrived.'

Princess Margaret merely sighed and said, 'Oh well, I suppose somebody had better offer her a drink.'

Years earlier in 1967, the Princess had described Elizabeth Taylor to playwright Emlyn Williams as 'a common little thing'.

Speaking on a primetime TV British chat show in 2016, actress Carrie Fisher claimed that her father Eddie Fisher, who had been Elizabeth Taylor's fourth husband from 1959–64, had a brief affair with Princess Margaret and that was the origin of the *froideur* between Taylor and the Princess.

When Richard Burton, Elizabeth Taylor's fifth (and sixth) husband, presented his wife with the huge Krupp diamond in 1968, Princess Margaret denounced it as 'the most vulgar thing I've ever seen', a comment that was widely reported.

Meeting at a party a short time after, Elizabeth Taylor was wearing the famous diamond as a ring. 'Ain't it great?' she asked the Princess, before convincing Margaret to try it on.

Once it was on the royal finger, Taylor commented, 'Doesn't look so vulgar now, does it?'

Although Margaret clearly had a sense of humour, it may have failed at times, when she was publicly teased. At a film premiere attended by Princess Margaret, Richard Burton announced to the audience, 'My name is really Richard Jenkins and up there is a lady whose name is Maggie Jones.' The Princess was not amused.

Novelist Christopher Isherwood met the Princess in Los Angeles in 1978, at a dinner party given by Kenneth Tynan. He was seated at her table but commented, 'Meeting Princess Margaret was hardly a dance. We only got her in very short hops …'

Afterwards, he said that she 'seemed quite a common little thing, fairly good-humored but no doubt quite capable of rapping your knuckles.' His verdict was reminiscent of the Princess's own earlier view of Elizabeth Taylor.

Meeting the great and good of Hollywood at another party during the same visit the Princess was seated next to Michael Caine. 'I already knew Princess Margaret, so I was considered socially safe enough to be seated at her right hand at the dinner table,' he remembered. However, also at the table was the Governor of California, Jerry Brown, who managed to completely offend the Princess.

'Good evening, Your Highness,' he began, horror of horrors, leaving out the 'Royal'. He then compounded matters by explaining that he had just 'dropped by' and would be leaving soon after the first course as he had another engagement, breaking the other taboo of leaving a formal occasion before the Princess. She immediately turned her back and ignored him.

The Governor's girlfriend, the singer Linda Ronstadt, then appeared. As the Princess's table was served first, the first course was already there. 'What are we having to start?' the singer asked. She leaned over to look at her boyfriend's meal, resting one hand on the Governor's shoulder and the other on Princess Margaret's. Michael Caine said, 'I have seen people shrug many times, but the Princess's shoulder shrugged like a punch from a boxer and with almost the same effect on Miss Ronstadt. She almost overbalanced and fell on the floor. At no point did Her Royal Highness even look up.'

Afterwards, the Princess told Michael Caine that she had enjoyed the evening, which had included dancing with John Travolta, 'But I didn't like that dreadful man at all.'

After throwing a party for Marlene Dietrich at Kensington Palace, Princess Margaret was appalled to find that a gift to her of four bottles of rare and expensive vodka had vanished. Determined not to let the matter drop, the Princess spent the next day telephoning everyone who had been there. The bottles were duly returned.

Closer to Home

Meeting Boy George in the 1980s at the height of his fame with Culture Club, Princess Margaret was unimpressed.

'I don't know who he is, but he looks like an over made-up tart. I refuse to be photographed with him. I'm too old for that sort of thing.'

In 1984, the Princess took part in an episode of BBC Radio 4's *The Archers* – the world's longest running radio soap about British country folk. Princess Margaret, playing herself, was supposed to be attending a fashion show in aid of her charity, the NSPCC, held at Grey Gables, the smart hotel in Ambridge where the show is set.

The Princess spoke her lines correctly, after which the producer tentatively suggested, 'Just wonderful. I just wonder if, when we do it one more time, you might give the impression that you were, well, enjoying yourself.'

The Princess looked completely baffled. 'Well, I wouldn't be, would I?' she said pointedly.

The Princess was never one to bother with faint praise or diplomatically non-committed verdicts. A fan of the ballet and a regular theatre- and film-goer, she had decided opinions. Some of her most cutting comments were directed at performances of one sort or another.

After the Royal Command Performance of the Oscar nominated *Love Story*, in 1970, Princess Margaret met the Paramount Studio chief and film's producer, Robert Evans. He remembered, 'All of us stood in a receiving line as Lord Somebody introduced us, one by one, to Her Majesty and her younger daughter. It was a hell of a thrill, abruptly ending when the lovely princess shook my hand. "Tony saw *Love Story* in New York. Hated it," she said.'

Drag artist Danny La Rue loathed latecomers to his act. One evening he noticed a woman leading a small group into his club. 'Good evening,' he shouted. 'Sorry, darling, I didn't recognise you with your clothes on.' It was only afterwards that he learned the woman was Princess Margaret. Luckily his brazen humour did not offend and she was to become a frequent visitor and got to know the entertainer well.

Commenting on the Princess, La Rue said she was 'witty and highly intelligent … you always knew you were in the presence of a princess.'

In the early seventies, the Princess was introduced to the TV and radio producer Dennis Main Wilson. At the time he was working on the long-running, popular British sitcom *Till Death Us Do Part* for the BBC. John Fortune, writing in the *New Statesman*, remembered that Margaret was dismissive. 'Isn't that that frightfully dreary thing in the East End?' she asked.

She was not a fan of the musical *Bow Down* by Harrison Birtwistle and Tony Harrison, which she saw at London's Cottesloe Theatre in July 1975 with Peter Hall, then Director of the esteemed National Theatre.

Hall wrote in his diary: 'A fairly disastrous evening. Princess Margaret was very affronted by the whole thing, and afterwards said she didn't think she should have been invited.' It seems that although she was not shocked by its theme, she did not think she should have attended such a controversial play as an official representative of the monarchy.

In 1986, actor Rupert Everett went to the theatre with Princess Margaret. Talking about the evening years later, he remembered his first mistake was failing to light her cigarette.

She may not have minded that much, as when she saw him getting into her car the Princess commented, 'Hey, you've got marvellous legs,' and proceeded to call Everett 'Leggy' all evening.

During the play's interval, the Princess grew impatient when the actor went to the bathroom, eventually going to collect him.

'She banged on the door and went, "Come on, Leggy!"' Everett explained. 'I spent the whole of the second act without having a pee. I never got asked again, I must say. She didn't realise that there were two princesses there; one of them was me.'

The Artistic Director of London's National Theatre, Richard Eyre, greeted Princess Margaret in the theatre foyer before escorting her in to watch a preview of Stephen Sondheim's *Sunday in the Park with George* in spring 1990.

He wrote: 'As she comes in she announces to me quite loudly that she can't *stand* Sondheim. She demonstrates this quite conspicuously throughout the evening. She raps me, quite painfully, and only half jokingly, at the end of the National Anthem, which Jeremy Sams has rearranged in a slightly arch fashion. She shifts restlessly during the show. At the interval, grim comedy getting her a drink. Ice! Whisky! Water! And more whisky. She wasn't hard work after the show. She talked to me about public speaking, which she hates ...'

A couple of years later, after watching a performance of the musical *Carousel* at the National Theatre, Richard Eyre dared to say to Princess Margaret, 'I'm so glad you enjoyed the show.'

The Princess looked blank. 'I didn't. I can't bear the piece.'

After the 1995 premiere at the Cottesloe Theatre, of playwright David Hare's *Skylight*, which is set in an East End London council flat, Princess Margaret was asked if she had found the new play depressing.

Rather mysteriously, she answered, 'It was a bit like one's own life.'

Never afraid to pass judgement even if it meant insulting people. She told Cecil Beaton that she 'loathed' Tennessee

Williams' plays, elaborating, 'I hate squalor! Tennessee Williams makes me feel ill!'

The Princess also loathed opera. She told National Theatre Director, Richard Eyre: 'Can't stand it. A lot of frightfully boring people standing still on stage and yelling.'

In 1980, when photographer Norman Parkinson decided to photograph the three Windsor women, the Queen, Queen Mother and Princess Margaret, together all wearing identical deep-blue satin capes, there were unforeseen difficulties. His directions of the usual, 'Turn to the right, ma'am', or 'Chin up a little, ma'am', simply led to confusion.

'It's absolutely no use you ma'aming us like this,' Margaret explained. 'We haven't the slightest idea who you are referring to. We are all ma'am.' The resulting photograph, taken in 1980, hangs in the National Portrait Gallery in London.

Princess Margaret garnered many diary notes over the years, partly because she lived during an age when it was normal for people to keep diaries, but also because of the characters of many of those with whom she mixed. A number of the journals were written with a view to later publication. Some of the comments are remarkably telling, offering an insight into Margaret's character and life. Others record incidents that could be open to interpretation. Some are glowing, many are more spiteful.

Several people who maintained a level of discretion during the Princess's lifetime, made further stories public following her death when they no longer feared losing her friendship or dreaded feeling the sting of her waspish tongue.

Art historian and famed British diarist Sir Roy Strong first met Princess Margaret at the very end of the 1960s and frequently detailed their meetings in his diaries.

Early on he commented, 'Princess Margaret is a strange lady, pretty, tough, disillusioned and spoilt. To cope with her I decided one had to slap back, which I did and survived.'

In 1975, he recorded that the Princess was 'in beaming mood, slimmer ... and rather marvellous'.

By 1980, Strong was criticising the state of her apartment at Kensington Palace as 'grubby and run-down', writing, 'It was awful to hear HRH droning on about how wonderful Anthony Blunt was but I've endured worse evenings with her.'

In 1982, he noted, 'No, she hadn't enjoyed the Gonzaga exhibition, the musical *The Mitford Girls* or the *Evening Standard* Drama Awards.'

By the following year he was relishing the gossip about Margaret's recent visit to Miami. No officials had been informed of her arrival, 'with the result that she was shunted through what we all endure. Bad temper resulted. Much funnier was when she had to walk through the arch which registers metal which she set off jangling like blazes. No one knew what to do because it had been set a-singing by the antiquated metal-supported corsetry she wore beneath!'

By the end of the decade he had taken to 'dodging' invitations.

In the 1970s, writer and critic Sacheverell Sitwell described a post-theatre dinner at the Italian Embassy, when Princess Margaret seemed intent on one of her infamous late nights:

'She kept on approaching the door, and just as we were encouraged to think she was really about to take her departure, she suddenly went back into the centre of the room and became engaged in animated conversation – all just to tease and annoy.'

Few were as openly venomous as diarist and Conservative party MP Alan Clark, who wrote on 10 June 1982: 'Fat, ugly, dwarf-like, lecherous and revoltingly tastelessly behaved Princess Margaret.'

In 1968, Cecil Beaton watched the Danish Ballet at Covent Garden – he described the ballet itself as 'agony' but was far more interested in Princess Margaret's appearance: 'Princess Margaret with an outrageous, enormous Roman matron head-do much too important for such a squat little figure … the common little Lord Snowdon, who was wearing his hair in a dyed quiff.'

Seeing the Princess at the ball before the wedding of Princess Anne and Captain Mark Phillips in 1973, Beaton took a malevolent delight when he wrote in his diary: 'Gosh the shock. She has become a little pocket monster – Queen Victoria … Poor brute, I do feel sorry for her. She was not very nice in the days when she was so pretty and attractive. She snubbed and ignored friends. But my God has she been paid out! Her eyes seem to have lost their vigour, her complexion is now a dirty negligee pink satin.'

In April 1992, Jessica 'Decca' Mitford wrote to writer Maya Angelou about her experience of Princess Margaret's hauteur:

I rather loathe the Royals, especially Princess M. Many years ago, Bob [Decca's American husband and radical lawyer] *and I were at a dinner party at Edna O'Brien's house – all sorts of actors etc. at dinner. After dinner, a new crowd came, Gore Vidal and followers, plus Princess M. The latter plunked herself next to me on a small love-seat in the drawing room. 'How's Debo* [Decca's sister Deborah, the Duchess of Devonshire]*?' she asked in her silly little voice … so I muttered, 'I suppose she's all right,' edging away. Bob comes over, so I say, 'This is my husband Bob Treuhaft.' Bob: 'Typical English introduction! What's your name?' Princess M. comes over all royal and says 'Decca, please present your husband to me.' 'I can't think why you can't simply SAY your name,' says I. So she calls over a sort of Gold Stick character to do it right. 'May I present Mr Treuhaft?' Such bosh, when she shows up with the Gore Vidal heavy drinking, heavy drugging set. When the princesses were little, I tried to spread a rumour in London that they'd been born with webbed feet which was why nobody had ever seen them with their shoes off; also, that Princess Lilibet (as Elizabeth was known by an adoring Brit. Public) was actually the Monster of Glamis …*

Another Mitford sister, the novelist Nancy, wrote an equally unflattering account of the Princess in a letter to her mother, sent from Paris in 1959. Margaret was notorious for being late for any and every occasion and made no exception for a dinner held in her honour:

'Dinner was at eight-thirty, and at eight-thirty Princess Margaret's hairdresser arrived, so we waited for hours while he concocted a ghastly coiffure … She looked like a huge ball of fur on two well-developed legs. Shortest dress I ever saw – a Frenchman said it begins so low and ends so soon.'

Mustique
Madness

Princess Margaret spent February 1955 on an official visit to the Caribbean. She was greeted warmly by crowds wherever she went and in her goodbye speech at the end of the trip she praised the wonderful mix 'of great fields of sugar cane, of golden beaches and towering palms, and of an azure sea forever studded with the sails of your graceful ships.'

It was a place that captured her heart and to which she would return again and again.

The Princess's first glimpse of Mustique, viewed from the deck of *Britannia*, was not favourable.

'The island looked like Kenya,' she recalled. 'Burnt to a frazzle. We drove down a path, the only road, and sat in the brush whacking mosquitoes.'

Colin Tennant – Lord Glenconner – one of the Princess's oldest friends, had three years earlier, bought the island on something of a whim for a snip at £45,000, though at the time it had neither fresh water nor electricity. Tennant suggested that the Princess and Lord Snowdon stop off there during their honeymoon. 'It's very primitive but it has magical beaches. Anne and I will be there, living in our hut, and we won't bother you at all.'

Wedding Present

Despite her less than positive first impressions, when Colin Tennant later asked what she would prefer as a wedding present, 'Would you like a bit of my island or something I can wrap up and send you?' the Princess didn't hesitate.

'A piece of land,' she told him.

She opted for a ten-acre plot on Mustique.

Tony, though, felt excluded from the offer. He had always despised Lord Glenconner, who he usually referred to as 'that shit', and never set foot on the island again.

Though she didn't visit Mustique again for years, as the state of her marriage to Tony declined, the Princess's interest in a plot of land there was revived. She invited herself back to stay with the Tennants on the island in 1968 and after some quibbling over boundaries, with stake posts literally being shifted back and forth by Colin Tennant and the Princess, Margaret claimed her ten acres. She also decided that Tony's uncle, the theatre designer Oliver Messel, would be the perfect candidate to design her a house. Perhaps she hoped to entice her increasingly absent husband out to stay on the island, or maybe this was simply another weapon and way to irritate him.

Les Jolies Eaux

Named *Les Jolies Eaux*, the house was finally completed and ready for Margaret in 1973. The name, meaning 'pretty waters', suggests the simplicity of the place. Colin Tennant described it as 'terribly plain' and said, 'There was a sofa facing the sea with a comfortable armchair on either side with a basketry kind of coffee table in front. There was no evidence at all of her being a royal person other than a rather small reproduction of the picture of the Queen by Annigoni which hung beside her desk.'

The Princess said of *Les Jolies Eaux*, 'I had always longed to build a house – with one's own ideas about cosy corners … It was great fun to do though difficult from a distance. I had to do it all from England … I put up a portrait of the Queen for people from abroad to see it's an English house.'

'Mustique is *my* country home,' she explained, adding, 'It is the only square inch of the world I own.'

It became her favourite place and a treasured escape.

Lord Snowdon never visited and always maintained that Colin Tennant exploited Margaret's presence there to promote his island among the jet set. Tennant himself stated that he lived 'by the three Ps – the People, the Press and the Princess'.

Royal Mustique

For the Princess, an average day on Mustique involved sun, sea and copious amounts of alcohol. For all the risqué rumours and suggestive press images, even there Margaret could never quite forget she was a princess, and she certainly never allowed anyone else to completely forget the fact either.

Although, as Colin Tennant said, Mustique 'was the first place, I suppose, where inhibitions could be cast off.'

One of her ladies-in-waiting explained: 'There were only fifteen houses on the island and everyone knew everyone else. Someone would have a house party one day and the next day someone else would have the whole island to lunch.'

As 'lord' of the island, Colin Tennant tried to ensure that Mustique was a safe haven, explaining, 'No outsiders were allowed in. If someone arrived on the plane I didn't approve of – like a journalist – then I would put them back on the plane and send them away. I was the arbiter of style and also the judge of who should be allowed to share it with us.' The centre of island life was Tennant's hotel, the Cotton House. 'I like to mix people. We mixed up the people from the village with the people who had built homes and the people from the palace and it worked. We had Mick Jagger and David Bowie and other fun-loving people there. It was one continuous party. Princess Margaret joined in everything and mixed with people there with whom she would never have contemplated socialising in London.'

It seems that Princess Margaret really did let down a few of her royal defences on Mustique, though she kept hold of her famously quick-fire humour: 'Would you mind awfully, ma'am, if I were to remove my swimming trunks,' Colin Tennant asked. It was the 1970s and there was something of a trend for stripping off.

'So long as I don't have to look at IT,' the Princess replied.

He proceeded to do so, persuading his friend Nicholas Courtney as well as Roddy Llewellyn to join him. Photographs of Margaret with the two men, her specially designed swimsuit's skirt preserving their dignity (just) were later to find their way into the newspapers, adding to the scandal and colourful headlines that surrounded the Princess's time in Mustique.

Party Island

Fancy dress parties were a regular feature of island life and Margaret's choice of costumes was revealing. She once made an unforgettable appearance wearing a Valkyrie outfit and proceeded to mime an aria from Wagner's *Ring* cycle.

Then for her fiftieth birthday party on Mustique, Colin and Anne Tennant gave her a gift of a gold, embroidered dress from India which really struck a chord with the Princess. She was absolutely delighted with the present.

'I've always LONGED to have a dress like that,' she exclaimed. 'It's what a REAL princess would wear.'

A poignant reminder that the royal rebel knew that her role was to be always that of the naughty younger sister confined to taking on the stand-in roles.

Travelling back and forth to Mustique, the Princess liked to joke that the initials for British West Indian Airways, the airline she often flew with to the Caribbean, actually stood for 'But Will It Arrive?'

Rumour and Scandal

Although the stories of Margaret's relationship with Roddy Llewellyn did not reach the newspapers until the leaked photograph of them together on the beach on Mustique was published in 1976, their closeness was no secret on the island. They got on so well at their first meeting at the Tennant's home in Scotland that the Princess soon after invited Llewellyn to be her guest at *Les Jolies Eaux*.

The torrent of revelations in the press about the Princess and her young lover holidaying at her Caribbean hideaway meant that he would be forever associated with her life there. The scandalised headlines tarnished her reputation for ever.

After a year, their clandestine relationship became too much for Llewellyn, who left to go travelling. With Snowdon embroiled in his own relationship with Lucy Lindsay-Hogg, Margaret found herself isolated and lonely.

Unable to sleep, she took too many sleeping tablets. The Princess, along with her friends, always denied this was a suicide attempt.

She explained, 'I was so exhausted because of everything that all I wanted to do was sleep … and I did, right through to the following afternoon.'

Llewellyn soon returned to London and the Princess. Their relationship continued for seven years and they remained friends for the rest of her life. When Roddy Llewellyn married Tatiana Soskin in 1981, it was with Margaret's blessing. She even hosted a lunch party for the couple to celebrate their engagement.

For a time the Princess was close to Old Etonian businessman Norman Lonsdale. He was a frequent visitor to Mustique and often escorted Margaret socially. She was forthright in her answer to press speculation that they were engaged:

'Absolute rubbish!' she responded.

When reports of a possible marriage persisted, focusing on a ring the Princess had been seen wearing on the third finger of her left hand, she said, 'When a fifty-one-year-old woman, the mother of a twenty-year-old son, puts a twenty-five-year-old ring on her finger, it does not mean she is going to get married.'

Nevertheless, she left the door tantalisingly open for future gossip by adding, 'Remarriage would be a devil of a trouble. And one would not want to be a bind. But if one did find someone nice ...'

The Princess and the Wide Boy

The newspapers were obsessed with the jet-set party lifestyle the Princess was said to lead on Mustique. One story that fired a frenzy of media speculation involved an actor and petty criminal called John Bindon. He was photographed with Princess Margaret on the island and at various times, whilst claiming to be totally loyal and discreet, claimed to have had an affair with her.

Most sources close to the Princess think an affair was extremely unlikely and that might have been the end of the matter, except for Bindon's notorious party trick. No one quite agrees on the details but he was able to balance or hang several beer glasses (five half-pint glasses of the old handled design) on his erect penis, as witnessed by a number of different people including Christine Keeler.

According to Bindon's biographer, Wensley Clarkson, at Colin Tennant's New Year's Eve Party in 1975, where the guests included Bryan Ferry, Jerry Hall and Mick Jagger, another of the party revellers said to Bindon, 'Ma'am knows all about your advantage in life and would really like to see it.'

Always happy to oblige, Bindon walked along the beach with Princess Margaret and a lady-in-waiting and proceeded to display the goods. When the three returned to the party, the Princess's lady-in-waiting commented, 'I've seen bigger.'

The Royal Reputation

Margaret moved in an arty set, particularly after her marriage to Antony Armstrong-Jones in 1960, but she was far more of a stickler for the correct royal protocol and formality than her sister the Queen. One of her major flaws was her inability to reconcile her love of all things bohemian with her royal status.

She insisted on being addressed as 'ma'am' (to rhyme with 'ham'), though her closest friends were allowed to call her 'ma'am darling'. As Margaret explained to actress Dana Gillespie who, meeting her on Mustique in the 1970s, asked what she should call her: 'Ma'am, just like a Christian name.' Even her husband and children were supposed to refer to her as Princess Margaret in front of visitors.

What's in a Name?

The Princess was Margaret only to the Queen and her cousin Margaret Rhodes, while the Queen Mother usually called her 'Darling', and she was Margot or Aunt Margot to the younger generation of royals. The only person outside the family who was allowed to call her Margaret was Ruby Gordon, her dresser since childhood.

> Margaret would rebuke anyone who dared
> miss the 'Royal' from 'Your Royal Highness',
> saying often, 'There are members of Arab states
> who are highnesses. I am a Royal one.'

The Princess was equally at pains to correct any misconceptions about her son's and daughter's positions.

'My children are not royal; they just happen to have the Queen for their aunt.'

She would remind David and Sarah that she, meanwhile, was royal.

Lord Snowdon was also keen to make the matter clear, 'I am not a member of the Royal Family, I am married to a member of the Royal Family.'

'It was to be her misfortune that the ordinary exploits of adolescence, the natural life of a healthy and vivacious girl, in her case made newspaper paragraphs, instead of being dismissed with a laugh,' Margaret's childhood nanny and governess, Crawfie, wrote when the Princess was just nineteen. It was to remain the case throughout her life.

Lady Cynthia Gladwyn, the wife of the British Ambassador to France in the 1950s, was a noted diarist. She wrote after the Princess visited Paris: 'Princess Margaret seems to fall between two stools. She wishes to convey that she is very much the Princess, but at the same time she is not prepared to stick to the rules if they bore or annoy her, such as being polite to people.'

Historian A.L. Rowse watched the twenty-six-year-old Princess at a Buckingham Palace garden party in 1956 and afterwards commented, 'Interesting to watch her face, bored, *mecontente*, ready to burst out against it all: a Duke of Windsor among the women of the Royal Family.'

The Royal Image

Princess Margaret commented on her public image: 'When my sister and I were growing up, she was made out to be the goody-goody one.' Adding, 'That was boring so the press tried to make out that I was wicked as hell.'

Gore Vidal wrote of a conversation he had with the Princess discussing her notoriety and difficult image.

'It was inevitable,' she said, 'when there are two sisters and one is the Queen, who must be the source of honour and all that is good, while the other must be the focus of the most creative malice, the evil sister.'

Her own opinion was, 'I'm no angel, but I'm no Bo-Peep either.'

Not surprisingly, the Princess came to resent her lack of privacy and the spotlight placed upon her every move.

'I have as much privacy as a goldfish in a bowl,' she observed.

She never felt the need to explain or justify herself, though, saying: 'I have no intention of telling people what I have for breakfast.'

'I have been misreported and misrepresented since the age of seventeen,' Princess Margaret has claimed more than once, giving an example of the first time she remembered a fabricated story appearing in the press:

'I was with some of my fellow Sea Rangers in a boat on the lake at Frogmore. And what do you think appeared in the newspapers? They said I had pulled the bung from the bottom of the boat! That made me frightfully cross. I was part of a team and very proud of it, I might tell you. I would never have dreamt of doing something so irresponsible.'

When asked why she thought she had been such a target for the press from a young age, the Princess replied, 'I was always told that it was because Lord Beaverbrook couldn't openly attack my father; my sister never did anything wrong – and anyway she married the right man – so he attacked me instead.' Press Baron Lord Beaverbrook founded the Express group of newspapers.

On BBC Radio 4's *Desert Island Discs*, in January 1981, Princess Margaret talked about her reaction to press stories about her life, 'I find them extremely aggravating. Of course, if they're absolutely invented, like sometimes they are, one can laugh at them with one's friends. But I think that since the age of seventeen, I've been misreported and misrepresented.' She added, 'They're not worth denying, really, because they're usually inaccurate.'

Looking back at the period of intense press scrutiny and criticism of her, particularly during the 1970s, Princess Margaret was philosophical, 'I had no way to retaliate. I just had to submit and keep quiet. They accused me of everything, and I did not have the chance to give an interview to put the record straight. All that is different now. Apart from taking my clothes off and bathing in the fountains of Trafalgar Square, I can do anything.'

Attending the re-opening of the restored Theatre Royal in Bath, the Princess was delighted to see the press photographers moved out of the way to allow her to pass:

'*Crunched* into a corner!' she exclaimed loudly as she walked by.

'Disobedience is my joy,' Margaret is said to have once asserted – possibly to Jean Cocteau, at a dinner party held at the British Embassy in Paris in April 1959.

She also stated, 'I have always had a dread of becoming a passenger in life.'

And on another occasion, 'I have no ambition. Isn't that terrible?'

'I am convinced I look ridiculous in a hat,' Princess Margaret once said.

The press and public's obsession with every aspect of Margaret's appearance continued throughout her life. As the years passed, the earlier admiration for her style and beauty, became increasingly critical, focusing on a morbid fascination with her weight and choice of clothes.

The Princess was resigned. 'People don't like me when I get fat, but I seem to have been alternately fat or thin on a two years' basis.' Asked how she managed to lose weight, she answered, stating the obvious, 'It's simple. I don't eat.'

Chroniclers of the Princess's life have, however, often noted that the happier she was in love, the less she weighed and the more glowing she appeared.

In the autumn of 1947, famed Parisian couturier Christian Dior showed his second collection at the Savoy Hotel in London. His acclaimed 'New Look' was so well received that the Queen Mother requested a private viewing the following day for members of the Royal Family, including Princess Margaret.

Dior wrote of the young Princess: 'She crystallised the whole popular frantic interest in royalty. She was a real fairy-tale princess, delicate, graceful, exquisite.'

The Princess subsequently visited the designer in Paris on many occasions and ordered a number of outfits, including the white ball gown in which she was photographed by Cecil Beaton for her twenty-first birthday in 1951, which she described as 'My favourite dress of all.'

'I never wore mini-skirts which were very high,' the Princess asserted.

Then another time, looking at an old photograph of herself wearing a mini, she commented, 'I can't believe I actually looked like that.'

Interviewed by her friend, the novelist Angela Huth, for a book called *The Englishwoman's Wardrobe*, in 1986, Princess Margaret explained:

'I always, always, have to be practical. I can't have skirts too tight because of getting in and out of cars and going up steps. Sleeves can't be too tight either; they must be all right for waving … I have very few home clothes, mostly working clothes. My working clothes are like most people's best clothes. I wear last year's for some private occasions, but they're too grand for the country.'

Princess Margaret was always sensitive about her lack of height and used to wear platform shoes and pile her hair on the top of her head to give the impression that she was taller than her real height of 5 feet 2 inches or 1.55m.

Actor and diarist Kenneth Williams wrote of the Princess's attitude to height in a letter to a friend in December 1975:

I saw Gordon Jackson [the actor] *in the canteen. He said he had been lunching with the Queen the day before. When he congratulated Princess Margaret on Snowdon's documentary about the midgets – 'The Little People' – she replied, 'not my cup of tea at all. Bit too near home I'm afraid' and he said, 'I suddenly realised, they're all tiny! The Queen, and Margaret, and the mum ....!'*

It was Barbara Skelton, the novelist and socialite, who first referred to Princess Margaret as 'the Royal Dwarf' in her diary entry for 2 December 1951, though Nancy Mitford also seems to have called her that. For Auberon Waugh, the Snowdons were 'the two highest paid performing dwarves in Europe'.

What's in a Word?

The Princess is said to have had strong views on words or phrases she considered vulgar, though her ideas of what was common seem to have been uniquely her own.

On hearing her host refer to the soup they were eating as 'Mulligatawny', Margaret insisted on correcting her. It was 'curried soup'.

She also disliked the term 'scrambled eggs', saying instead, 'We call them "buttered eggs".'

In his book *Ma'am Darling*, Craig Brown records two versions of the same story, one told by the Princess's long-time friend, Nicky Haslam, and the other by Peter Coats, then editor of *House and Garden Magazine*. Whichever version you choose to believe, the gist remains the same:

Bored at a house party, and 'mildly' arguing with his wife, Lord Snowdon began flicking matches in Margaret's direction. When one landed alight in her lap, the Princess brushed it away and asked him to stop before he set fire to her brocade dress. 'Good thing, too,' he replied. 'I hate that material.' At which point Margaret became icily pompous and in Coats' story snapped, 'Material is a word we do not use,' and in Haslam's version, stated, 'We call it stuff.'

Perhaps simply a little intolerant of listening to those discussing their children's unique talents, or from a desire never to be outdone, Princess Margaret once silenced some other parents boasting of their children's first words with, 'My boy's first word was "chandelier".'

Ma'am's Driver

Princess Margaret never learned to drive and instead always employed a personal driver. For the last twenty-six years of her life that was David Griffin, who answered a newspaper advert for a royal chauffeur in 1976.

Griffin said of his time with the Princess: 'She was part of the old school and she never changed from day one. She was very starchy, no jokey conversation. She called me Griffin and I called her Your Royal Highness.' He added that the pair exchanged no more than polite greetings. Griffin said, 'A proper royal servant is never seen and never heard. We preferred to work in total silence, so we didn't have to be friendly. We never used to try and chat. They used to say Princess Margaret could freeze a daisy at four feet by just looking at it.

'Reflecting back, it was the best method of doing things. Princess Margaret was captain of the ship and she was a remarkable person. She could be difficult and she could be kind but you knew where you were with her. All her staff had been with her twenty years or more when she died. We would sometimes curse her, but we were always loyal.'

Griffin would get up early every day and would always polish the cars inside as well as out. He described a typical day:

'Mid-morning, I'd drive the Princess to the hairdresser's. Then she would go out for lunch at a nice restaurant. Then she'd come back to the Palace and have a rest. Then she'd go to the hairdresser's for the second time in one day. Then I'd drive her to pre-theatre drinks, then to the theatre, then post-theatre dinner. And I'd finish about three am. Sometimes this would happen every night. And I'd always be up at eight am. At the weekend, I'd drive her to the country. If she travelled to Europe, I'd get there first and pick her up at the airport in Prague, for example, so she never thought anything was different.'

The Princess had a number of different cars, including a Rolls-Royce Silver Wraith which had the floor specially raised to make her look taller, a Mercedes Benz 320 for private use, a small Daihatsu, and a Ford transit minibus to ferry friends around. 'Six or seven people would pile in and shout: "Orf we go on our outing."'

Like many Palace servants, Griffin was far from posh and he remembered Margaret taking a dim view of any who tried to speak with a more clipped accent.

'What on earth is wrong with him?' she would ask loudly, rolling her eyes.

One story about the Princess at a New York function has it that she dropped her coat. When a man immediately offered to pick it up for her, Margaret responded, 'No. I'll never remember where it is if you move it.'

Princess of Many Parts

Princess Margaret's talents as a mimic continued throughout her life. Her old friend, the columnist and royal biographer Kenneth Rose, wrote, 'The Princess shone as a mimic. She would recall Dame Joan Sutherland greeting her backstage after her sleepwalking scene from *Lucia di Lammermoor*: "Oi'm always meeting yew in moi nightie."'

> Biographer Michael Holroyd, sitting next to the Princess at a dinner party, heard her imitating their fellow guest, author Edna O'Brien's Irish brogue. She followed it with another impersonation that Holroyd could not quite place. He laughed and said, 'I think that's your funniest yet.' Met by stony silence he only then realised that Princess Margaret had been speaking in her own voice.

The writer Lady Caroline Blackwood remembered Princess Margaret at the beginning of the 1950s. They were both guests at a formal London ball given by Lady Rothermere, the celebrated hostess who later married Ian Fleming. She immediately spotted the Princess 'being worshipped by her adoring set who were known at the time as "the Smarties". She was revered and considered glamorous because she was the one "Royal" who was accessible. Princess Margaret smoked, and she drank, and she flirted.

She went to nightclubs and she loved showbusiness and popular music.'

Towards the end of the evening, during which the champagne had been flowing freely, the Princess 'grabbed the microphone from the startled singer of the band and she instructed them to play songs by Cole Porter.' The guests stopped dancing to watch.

'They shouted and they roared and they asked for more,' recalled Lady Caroline. 'Princess Margaret became a little manic at receiving such approval ... and she started wriggling around in her crinoline and tiara ... Her dress was unsuitable for this slinky act.'

The applause continued and the Princess was about to embark on 'Let's Do It' when the sound of loud booing and jeers erupted from the back of the ballroom. The Princess faltered. Mortified, she blushed scarlet and then turned pale, before fleeing from the microphone.

The heckling came from the painter, Francis Bacon. He had been blind drunk but was unrepentant. He later said, 'Her singing was really too awful. Someone had to stop her.'

Princess Margaret was frequently questioned about her musical abilities and admitted, 'I once composed a lament, words as well as music. That was after Peter Townsend and I knew we couldn't get married.'

At the end of her appearance on *Desert Island
Discs* in 1981, Princess Margaret was asked to
name her luxury item. She chose a piano.

Author and columnist, Christopher Hitchens, recalled his
own experience with the Princess during the 1970s. He
wrote in the *London Review of Books*: 'Two members of
the *New Left Review* ... were confronted by her at some
do or another. It was the fashion in those days to address
everybody as "man", and they concluded later that HRH
hadn't objected to this informality because she thought
they were saying "ma'am". I myself cannoned into her,
flesh-tinted and well into the gin (her, I mean), as I entered
a cocktail party. She was unescorted, and seized on me as a
new arrival.

'"Know anything about china?" she demanded.

'I truly did not know whether she meant porcelain or
the Middle Kingdom, and was very grateful for whatever
rescue eventuated. There she was, I mean to say, going
around the place letting in daylight on magic like billy-oh.'

Princess Margaret had an extensive collection of seashells
which she had accumulated on her travels around the world
and displayed in special glass cabinets in her apartment
at Kensington Palace. The Natural History Museum in

London described it as 'one of the most comprehensive shell collections in individual ownership'. It may be an unlikely image, but when she was bored, the Princess enjoyed taking out the shells and polishing them.

Food, Booze and Cigarettes

The Princess had some very definite ideas as far as eating and drinking went. She was a fan of picnics, but only when they were planned to her exacting standards.

'Nearly all picnics in the country end up, in desperation, in a lay-by because no one can decide where to stop. In my opinion, picnics should always be eaten at a table, sitting on a chair.'

'We both hated black-tie and when we invited friends to dinner, the men always asked what they should wear,' the Princess said of entertaining with her husband Lord Snowdon. 'We said anything but black-tie, and they always came in the most beautiful shirts.'

Margaret's friend, Kenneth Rose, described her tastes in food as 'luxurious simplicity'.

'She ate very little, rarely meat,' he said. 'Although game and some fish were acceptable, she would wave away a dish of gleaming salmon trout, demand an omelette, ask if she could exchange it for a boiled egg which in its turn was rejected as too hard or too soft … Hosts and hostesses never forgot the princess who came to dinner …'

The Princess disliked potatoes, and if she refused a dish, no one else was allowed to have it either. Hosts knew to serve her first and the meal was over the minute the Princess put down her knife and fork. As she tended to eat very little and very fast, fellow diners were often left hungry, with half-eaten meals remaining on their plates.

She once asserted, 'My vices are cigarettes and drink. And I don't see myself giving those up.'

It was said that during the 1950s and 60s when the convention was that no one was allowed to smoke until the royal toast had been made at the end of a meal, Princess Margaret would ensure the toast was said after the first course.

The Princess always used a distinctive, long holder for her cigarettes, which she carried in a green leather case.

There were thirty-seven smoking-related items amongst her personal possessions auctioned at Christie's after her death. Her reputation as a smoker ensured that often gifts from foreign dignitaries were ashtrays, cigarette cases or lighters.

Guests to *Les Jolies Eaux* or Kensington Palace would all remark on how much she drank, 'Yet she never seemed to get drunk.' Her drink of choice was originally gin and tonic, but she switched to whisky, of which her favourite was Famous Grouse, and which she liked with bottled Malvern mineral water, never tap.

Former footman David Payne noted, 'Chief object of her scrutiny was the special bottle of sealed Malvern water … which the Princess insisted on taking with her Scotch whisky.' Should hosts dare to offer anything else, she argued on many occasions, 'That is not water. It is only tap water!'

A frequent guest at Kensington Palace noted, 'She hardly touched her food … but she smoked almost non-stop. A silver cigarette box and an ashtray were beside her plate and she was forever discarding one filter from her long holder and replacing it with a new one.'

> Playwright Keith Waterhouse noticed the ash on Princess Margaret's cigarette growing longer and longer at a party in the 1980s. He reached across her, palm upwards, intending to grab an ashtray. 'She simply flicked her ash into my open palm as it passed,' he remembered. 'Thank God she hadn't decided to stub it out.'

When Lord Carnarvon gave her a glass of his rare and very valuable 1836 Madeira, Princess Margaret took a sip and condemned it as tasting, 'Exactly like petrol.'

When questioned why she never offered anyone else a light, the Princess replied, 'Every time I lend my lighter, somebody pinches it.'

After watching British actor Derek Jacobi onstage as Richard II, Princess Margaret invited him to join her and some friends at Joe Allen's restaurant in Covent Garden, London.

Jacobi recalled: 'There were eight of us and I sat next to her. She smoked continuously, not even putting out her cigarette when the soup arrived, but instead leaning it up against the ashtray. We got on terribly well, very chummy, talking about her mum and her sister, and she really made me feel like I was a friend, until she got a cigarette out and I picked up a lighter and she snatched it out of my hand and gave it to a ballet dancer called David Wall.

'"You don't light my cigarette, dear. Oh no, you're not that close."'

Journalist and broadcaster Derek Jameson met Princess Margaret at the Earl's Court Boatshow. Jameson, himself a keen smoker, noticed the Princess smoking untipped Players. He commented, 'That's a rough old fag you've got there, ma'am.'

'What do you mean?' Margaret asked.

'Well, they're plain and very strong. You'll do yourself a mischief smoking those. Top of the coffin nail league,' he replied.

But the Princess knew better, 'No, they're not. Capstan Full Strength are worse.'

The pair went on to discuss the merits of different brands and how impossible it was to give up smoking.

In the end, ill health was to force her hand to stop smoking at the turn of the new century, although even then it is likely that although she drastically cut down, she never quite entirely stopped.

Not a Fan

Princess Margaret was apparently not a fan of Princess Michael, wife of her cousin, Prince Michael of Kent. During a traditional carriage procession at Ascot in which she was forced to sit beside Princess Michael, she would answer the latter's chatter with a grudging grunt. Afterwards, Margaret demanded of the Queen, 'Why did you put me next to that woman?'

Her sister replied calmly, 'Because I knew that it would give you a chance to do what you like best … Concentrate on the two attractive men sitting opposite.'

When asked about rumours that Princess Michael was moving to America, she replied, 'Yes, we thought we'd got rid of her.'

> Princess Michael has had various nicknames
> among members of the Royal Family, none very
> flattering, including Princess Pushy, Princess Porky,
> Rent-a-Princess, the Valkyrie and Our Val.

Former Comptroller of the Lord Chamberlain's Office, Johnny Johnston, asserted of the Princess, 'When she was nice, she was very, very nice. When she was awkward, she was very awkward. I always felt that her view was: "There's no need to be nice to this chap. He works for my sister."'

Uniquely Margaret

Contemporary of the Queen and lifelong family friend, Prue Penn, said her abiding memory of Margaret was of laughter. 'At a dinner party, she'd catch my eye and we'd get the giggles until the tears ran down our faces. We couldn't stop. She was a great giggler.'

Her lady-in-waiting and wife of her old friend Colin Tennant, Anne Tennant, Lady Glenconner agreed, 'I just remember Princess Margaret being tremendously vivacious, and fun, and roaring with laughter. People said her life was a sad one, but I don't think it was.'

Other friends talk of her willingness to help with washing dishes and generally lending a hand. She liked simple kitchen suppers with people she knew well and intelligent chat. It was when she felt she was being 'shown off' or exhibited, when extras were suddenly invited to dinner or weekend parties that she would pull rank and act the Princess, making extravagant demands.

The Loyal Princess

Lady Elizabeth Cavendish, lady-in-waiting to the Princess and long-time friend, said, 'I know that no matter what I had done, she would have been there. The people who knew her best were devoted to her. She was, I think, the most loyal person I have ever met and, of course, to me a wonderful friend.'

She also said, in a similar vein, 'She is probably the loyalist friend you could have, once she's decided she likes you.'

Many have commented on the Princess's loyalty to her friends. She saw this as one of the ways in which she differed from her ex-husband, 'When we were married I pressed him to keep up with his old chums, but the funny thing about Tony is that he is a friend-dropper. After the marriage nearly all his old friends vanished and I never saw them again. I'm not like that, I don't discard people. My friends are old friends.'

The Human Princess

'Princess Margaret's "faults" are the indulgences of many human beings who are not absolute bores. She has a taste for booze and fags – who hasn't?' A.N. Wilson said in 1997.

Although another of her friends and occasional dates in later life admitted, 'She can be unbelievably rude. Quite takes your breath away.'

Interior designer Nicky Haslam, a personal friend of the Princess from childhood, said, 'She was an original; not afraid to cast her opinion and say what she thought. She could be delightfully critical and fiercely intellectual.'

Is it any wonder that the Princess's behaviour was seen as inconsistent? Writer and journalist Selina Hastings came to know Princess Margaret fairly well for a time from the late 1970s, particularly after the breakdown of the Princess's marriage to Lord Snowdon. Like Gore Vidal, she thought people tended to underestimate Margaret, commenting on the Princess's childhood, 'On one side she was given an inflated sense of her own value, while on the other her confidence was continually undermined by comparisons with her sister; she was very spoilt and indulged and made to feel a very special person indeed, while simultaneously being given clearly to understand that it was her sister who was important.'

Selina Hastings was also impressed by how considerate the Princess was towards her:

'She was … always very, very nice. I was so touched that she had gone to the trouble to organise something that would interest me. She was more intelligent than a lot of people give her credit for: she used to go once a week to the V&A and she'd just concentrate on one object. When she went to New York, she knew exactly what she wanted to see, and she'd go to galleries and museums. Once when she visited New York, her host asked her what she would like to do, thinking that she'd want to go to Bloomingdale's or Saks. Instead she chose to be taken to the Pierpont Morgan Library to look at the medieval missals. It turned out she knew almost as much about them as the curator did.'

Princess Margaret could, perhaps understandably, be strangely detached from normal life. She once asked Selina Hastings if she ever used Carmen rollers and if so, where did one buy them? On being told, Boots the chemist, Princess Margaret exclaimed, 'No! How too fascinating!'

Royal Reading

The Princess took a great interest in reading anything that appealed to her, though she had literary taste in books. Biographer Tim Heald discovered that she had read Colin Thubron's novels rather than his more accessible travel books and was generally well informed. She became fascinated by the nineteenth-century poet Coleridge after reading Richard Holmes' 1989 biography. Realising that the helicopter she was in was passing close to the poet's former home at Nether Stowey in Somerset, the Princess asked the pilot to detour and fly low over the house so that she could take a look.

Novelist and friend Angela Huth remembered Margaret coming to stay with her and her husband after they moved to Oxford in 1978:

'She particularly liked to see Dame Iris Murdoch … she loved listening to Iris talk about philosophy, retaining all she could. Each time a new Murdoch novel appeared she would pounce upon it, but, to my amazement, she also made headway into Iris's last tome on philosophy. "I had to read it with the *Encyclopaedia Britannica* beside me," she confessed. "It was difficult, but worth the effort.'"

Kensington
Palace

At the beginning of 1985, Princess Margaret had a serious lung operation and, although she thought she never would, attempted to give up smoking. Some 2000 cigarettes were returned. As part of her recovery, the Princess also swapped the Famous Grouse for Robinson's Barley Water. The change was temporary. Within months she was said to be smoking thirty cigarettes a day; admittedly a big reduction on the rumoured sixty that had previously been her habit.

Standing Down

It was around this time that she lost her place on the list of members of the Royal Family eligible to act as Counsellors of State if the Queen was away or incapacitated.

Queen Elizabeth's youngest son Prince Edward had now come of age and as Sir William Heseltine, the Queen's Private Secretary, explained, '… the Counsellors are to be Prince Philip and Queen Elizabeth the Queen Mother and the four persons next in the line of succession, not disqualified by age. So, as her nephews and niece came of age Princess Margaret was knocked off the list.'

This news was greeted with disappointment by some. In a letter to Lord Napier, Princess Margaret's Private Secretary,

William Heseltine wrote, 'I know that both my colleagues here at Buckingham Palace will be sad to register this fact since Princess Margaret has always been so very kind and helpful whenever she has acted in that capacity, and we have depended on her for so many years.'

Privately, the Princess was upset. She had loved her duties as Counsellor of State. Publicly commenting on her nephews and niece coming of age, the Princess jokingly said, 'When the young ones grow up, old Auntie won't be needed.'

The Younger Generation of Royals

By the 1990s, Princess Margaret was no longer considered shocking. The press and paparazzi now focused their attention on the younger royals, in particular Prince Charles and Princess Diana, as well Andrew and Fergie – the Duke and Duchess of York.

'They all leave me alone these days,' the Princess commented. 'They've got other fish to fry.'

'Margot' and Diana

Speaking about her aunt by marriage, Princess Diana said, 'I've always adored Margot.' She later also told a friend,

'I love her to bits and she's been wonderful to me from day one.'

Indeed, the effect Diana had on the press and public was often likened to that of Princess Margaret in her twenties and thirties, and Margaret herself accepted the comparison: 'The Princess of Wales said all the things I was saying twenty-five years ago,' she said. 'Clothes aren't her prime concern. They weren't mine. But the fashion writers insist on treating her, as they did me, as if we were just unreal figures straight from *Dynasty*.'

Diana and Margaret seemed to understand one another – that is until it became obvious that Diana had collaborated closely on Andrew Morton's book *Diana: Her True Story*. Princess Margaret did not approve. At all. She sent Diana a furious note.

She also commented more than once, 'Poor Lilibet and Charles have done everything they can to get rid of the wretched girl, but she just won't go.'

After Diana's interview with Martin Bashir was broadcast in November 1995, Princess Margaret refused to have anything more to do with her. She totally ignored Diana, not an easy feat as they lived in neighbouring apartments in Kensington

Palace, though Margaret had years of practice ignoring her other neighbour there, Princess Michael.

Margaret's son, David Linley, working on his sports car outside the Palace, would dutifully duck out of sight if he saw Diana coming.

The public's emotional outpouring of grief after Diana's death, merely added to Margaret's distaste. Her lady-in-waiting Anne Tennant claimed, 'She didn't like the emotionalism one bit. She said the hysteria was rather like Diana herself. It was as if when she died she got everyone to be as hysterical as she was.'

When it was suggested that the statue of King William III outside Kensington Palace should be replaced with one of Princess Diana, Princess Margaret was appalled. She led the opposition to the scheme saying, 'I'm not having that woman outside my bedroom window.'

Margaret and Sarah

Margaret's relationship with Prince Andrew's wife, Sarah Ferguson, had probably never been particularly warm. Their characters were not really compatible and the Princess might well have found the new Duchess overly bouncy and a little vulgar. The fact that the Duchess of York now ranked ahead of her in the royal order of precedence would also have rankled.

Any effort at civility from Margaret towards the Duchess of York ceased when photographs that were splashed across the tabloids in 1992 showed the Duchess sunbathing topless, her big toe apparently being sucked by her 'financial adviser' John Bryan. This made anything salacious that had previously been published about Princess Margaret look positively innocent. She was outraged.

'She was more furious than I have ever seen her and that is saying something,' said a friend. The Queen passed her sister's strongly expressed opinion on to the Duchess who sent Margaret a note of apology together with a bouquet of flowers.

In return, the Princess sent her a handwritten reply:

Not once have you hung your head in embarrassment even for a minute after those disgraceful photographs. You have done more to bring shame on the Family than you could ever have imagined. Clearly you have never considered the damage you are doing to us all. How dare you discredit us like this and how dare you send me those flowers.

After Margaret's letter to the Duchess was leaked to the newspapers and published widely, Margaret was heard to murmur, 'My poor sister …' many times.

Following the erstwhile Duchess's departure from the Royal Family, Princess Margaret took over many of her duties. In many cases it was a resumption of a role that had previously been hers, rather than a new one.

The Children

In comparison with their Windsor cousins, Princess Margaret's own two children appear remarkably grounded as grown-ups. They are both long-married and have had flourishing careers.

Her friend and lady-in-waiting Lady Elizabeth Cavendish said once, 'In her odd, detached way she's been a very good mother. Against all the odds.' As parents, the Snowdons made a good combination and Lady Sarah had often accompanied her mother on official overseas trips as a teenager.

'I don't think it's essential to be at the christening of your nephew's children,' the Princess said somewhat defensively, to excuse her absence from both Prince Charles' and Prince Andrew's children's christenings.

Of Princess Anne, with whom she came to share a close bond, she commented, 'Anne's more positive than I was.

She's much tougher, too, she's been brought up in a different atmosphere.'

Like her aunt, Princess Anne had married and divorced a commoner, was independent, prone to speaking her mind, and didn't suffer fools gladly. When Anne was younger, Margaret would give her advice on public appearances and what to wear.

Final Years

Princess Margaret would sometimes quip that the ill health that had dogged her since the 1970s was a result of her poor treatment by Lord Snowdon before their divorce, but aside from the likely impact on her health of her smoking, in truth she had always suffered from throat infections, laryngitis and bronchitis, as well as migraines.

She was hospitalised with hepatitis at the time Lord Snowdon told her he wanted a divorce, in May 1978, following their two years of separation. The divorce was finalised in July that year. Still convalescing, the Princess then embarked on an official tour of the South Pacific in September. The heavy schedule proved too much and she became extremely ill, this time with viral pneumonia. Her tendency was to carry on and make light of any health issues, but even she admitted, 'I very nearly died.'

The lung operation in 1985 was prompted by a cancer scare and a section of her left lung was removed. Tests proved benign and she appeared to make a good recovery. A mild stroke in 1998 also seemed to have little major impact on her spirits.

At the beginning of 1999, Princess Margaret badly scalded her feet in the shower in her house on Mustique.

No one really knows exactly what happened, but the Princess apparently confused the controls and sent jets of boiling water pouring over her feet. Staff found her in shock, though she refused to admit the severity of the injury and even after she was flown home to Balmoral to recuperate, would not agree to the skin grafts that she really needed, until it was too late.

Margaret spent six months convalescing after her accident, but afterwards was able to walk only a few steps. She took to using a wheelchair, which initially her sister considered unnecessary.

At a reception held at Windsor Castle to celebrate her mother's 100th birthday on 21 June 2000, Margaret spotted the unoccupied wheelchair carefully positioned in readiness for the Queen Mother and hopped into it. The Queen was not amused and snapped, 'For God's sake, Margaret, get out! That's meant for Mummy!'

For a time, when out visiting anywhere with her mother, Princess Margaret would effectively race her to the waiting wheelchair.

A series of strokes beginning in early 2001, meant a wheelchair was no longer an indulgence but a necessity. The Princess lost the sight in one eye and was largely paralysed on the left side of her body. She was extremely depressed and refused to see many people, sometimes not even her mother. The news that her son, Viscount Linley, to whom she had transferred ownership of her Mustique home a few years earlier as a wedding present, had sold *Les Jolies Eaux* only added to her feelings that life was no longer worth living.

The Princess soon told her lady-in-waiting and friend, Anne Tennant, that she would see no more men: 'I look so awful now – I don't want them to remember me like this.'

Roddy Llewellyn was one of her last male visitors.

Margaret's longstanding friend, Prue Penn, used to sit with her in her bedroom and read aloud to the Princess; Prue recalled Margaret as still defiantly demanding:

'She'd sit in the bedroom looking utterly miserable. The things she asked me to read … there was a Trollope.

A frightfully dull book. No men came at all. She couldn't bear to be seen by men. When she went to sleep, I stopped reading.

"I'll go, nurse," I'd say. "She's asleep."

"I'm not," she'd say.'

On Saturday 9 February 2002, Buckingham Palace announced the news that Princess Margaret had died. The Queen, Margaret's sister and protector, conveyed her feelings about Margaret's death through the official statement. Famous for her dignified restraint, Elizabeth II's sadness at her younger sister's passing is clear:

> *The Queen, with great sadness, has asked for the*
> *following announcement to be made immediately.*
> *Her beloved sister, Princess Margaret,*
> *died peacefully in her sleep this morning at*
> *6.30 in the King Edward VII Hospital.*

The then Prime Minister, Tony Blair, who was flying to Sierra Leone, made a broadcast from his plane: 'I'm deeply saddened to hear of the death of Princess Margaret. My thoughts are with the Queen, Queen Elizabeth the Queen Mother and the rest of the Royal Family at this time.'

A Royal Funeral

The Princess had been planning for her own funeral for some time. At one point she told a friend, 'I rather think I should like to be buried at sea.'

This was a passing notion, but she was constantly reviewing the details. 'I am always altering the arrangements for my funeral. I drive the Lord Chamberlain's Department mad,' she explained with some satisfaction to her old friend Kenneth Rose.

In the opinion of writer and royal historian Hugo Vickers, 'She was nicer than she thought she was.' Writing in the *Independent*, he speculated: 'The absence of a role was her tragedy … [her] slightly forbidding exterior concealed a kind heart. She moved in a society which relished feuds and firm loyalties – her friends were, in principle, her friends for life, but she was a naughty enemy … Close friends learned to be wary of her ways. At the moment that everyone was relaxing, she would surreptitiously resume her royal rank and reduce some helpless guest to dust.'

Sir Roy Strong was unconvinced. He wrote after her death in his diaries: 'It is a curious fact that if she had died in the middle of the 1960s, the response would have been akin to that on the death of Diana. As it was, she lived long enough

for the bitter truth about her to become general knowledge …
This was a princess who never seemed to think of anything
other than everyone's role to fulfil her slightest whim. All of
this was so sad because, when young, she had been beautiful,
vivacious and at times quick-witted.'

Many obituaries of the Princess opened with compliments
but went on to catalogue the trickier aspects of her character
and behaviour. Others emphasised her wasted potential and
the *Daily Telegraph* hit on a familiar theme: 'She had talents
and qualities which might, perhaps, have blossomed more
fully away from the constant blaze of publicity.'

'She was a multi-faceted and brilliant person with an
underlying simplicity and strength. She fascinated generation
after generation,' Lord St John of Fawsley, another old friend,
wrote. 'I have got wonderful memories of her. She was the
most beautiful debutante of her generation and she kept that
beauty right through her life. She was highly intelligent. In
many ways, she was one of the most intelligent women, one
of the cleverest women, I have ever met, and she never really
had an outlet for that intelligence. She had a turbulent life, of
course, but at the close of her life – in the last decade – she

had somehow "come into port". She was not at all unhappy. She loved her royal duties and she did them tremendously professionally.'

Prince Charles called her his 'darling aunt' and in a glowing tribute said, 'I think one of the fondest memories I shall have of her was of her sitting at the piano playing away with a large, very elegant cigarette holder in her mouth.' He also acknowledged, 'She had such a wonderfully free spirit and she absolutely loved life and lived it to the full …'

The final word, though, should go to the Princess. When pressed as to whether she would have liked her life to have been different, Princess Margaret was adamant:

'I cannot imagine anything more wonderful than to be who I am.'

Picture Credits

Bibliography

Amis, Kingsley, *Memoirs*, Hutchinson, 1991

Aronson, Theo, *Princess Margaret. A Biography*, Michael O'Mara Books, 1997

Arscott, David, *Queen Elizabeth II Diamond Jubilee 60 Years a Queen: A Very Peculiar History*, Book House, 2012

Beaton, Cecil, *Beaton in the Sixties*, Alfred A. Knopf, 2004

Beaton, Cecil, *The Unexpurgated Beaton Diaries*, ed. Hugo Vickers, Weidenfeld & Nicolson, 2002

Bedell Smith, Sally, *Elizabeth the Queen*, Penguin Books, 2012

Botham, Noel, *Margaret, The Last Real Princess*, Blake Publishing, 2002

Botham, Noel, and Montague, Bruce, *The Book of Royal Useless Information*, John Blake Publishing, 2012

Bricusse, Leslie, *Pure Imagination! A Sorta Biography*, Faber, 2015

Brown, Craig, *Ma'am Darling. 99 Glimpses of Princess Margaret*, 4th Estate, 2017

Caine, Michael, *What's It All About?* Arrow Books, 2010

Courtenay, Nicholas, *Lord of the Isle: The Extravagant Life and Times of Colin Tennant*, Bene Factum Publishing, 2012

Crawford, Marion, *The Little Princesses*, Cassell, 1950

Coward, Noel, *The Noel Coward Diaries*, ed. Graham Payne and Sheridan Morley, Weidenfeld & Nicolson, 1982

De Courcy, Anne, *Snowdon: The Biography*, Weidenfeld & Nicolson, 2008

Dempster, Nigel, *HRH The Princess Margaret: A Life Unfulfilled*, Quartet Books, 1981

Edwards, Anne, *Royal Sisters*, William Morrow & Co, 1990

Evans, Robert, *The Kid Stays in the Picture*, Hyperion Books, 1994

Eyre, Richard, *National Service: Diary of a Decade*, Bloomsbury, 2003

Giuliano, Geoffrey, *Dark Horse: The Secret Life of George Harrison*, Bloomsbury, 1989

Gladwyn, Cynthia, *The Diaries of Cynthia Gladwyn*, ed. Miles Jebb, Constable, 1995

Heald, Tim, *Philip: A Portrait of the Duke of Edinburgh*, William Morrow & Co, 1991

Heald, Tim, *Princess Margaret, A Life Unravelled*, Weidenfeld & Nicolson, 2007

James, Paul, *Margaret: A Woman of Conflict*, Sidgwick & Jackson, 1990

Jameson, Derek, *The Last of the Hot Metal Men*, Ebury Press, 1990

Lascelles, Sir Alan, *King's Counsellor: Abdication and War*, ed. Duff Hart-Davis, Weidenfeld & Nicolson, 2006

Lees-Milne, James, *A Mingled Measure: Diaries 1953–1972*, John Murray, 1994

Marr, Andrew, *Diamond Queen: Elizabeth II and Her People*, Macmillan UK, 2011

Mitford, Jessica, *Decca: The Letters of Jessica Mitford*, ed. Peter Sussman, Weidenfeld & Nicolson, 2006

Mitford, Nancy, *Love from Nancy: The Letters of Nancy Mitford*, ed. Charlotte Mosley, Hodder & Stoughton, 1993

Petrella, Kate, *Royal Wisdom: The Most Daft, Cheeky, and Brilliant Quotes from Britain's Royal Family*, Adams Media, 2011

Rhodes, Margaret, *The Final Curtsey*, Birlinn Ltd and Umbria Press, 2012

Rose, Kenneth, *Kings, Queens and Courtiers*, Weidenfeld & Nicolson, 1985

Shawcross, William, *Queen Elizabeth the Queen Mother: The Official Biography*, Macmillan, 2009

Sinclair, Marianne and Litvinoff, Sarah, *The Wit & Wisdom of the Royal Family*, Plexus Publishing, 1990

Strong, Roy, *The Roy Strong Diaries 1967–1987*, Weidenfeld & Nicolson, 1997

Sussman, Peter, ed., *Decca: The Letters of Jessica Mitford*, Weidenfeld & Nicolson, 2006

Townsend, Peter, *Time and Chance: An Autobiography*, Collins, 1978

Tynan, Kenneth, *The Diaries*, ed. John Lahr, Bloomsbury, 2001

Vickers, Hugo, *Elizabeth the Queen Mother*, Hutchinson, 2005

Vidal, Gore, *Palimpsest: A Memoir*, Andre Deutsch, 1995

Vidal, Gore, *Snapshots in History's Glare*, Harry N. Abrams, 2009

Walker, Alexander, *Elizabeth: The Life of Elizabeth Taylor*, Grove Press, 2001

Warwick, Christopher, *Princess Margaret. A Life of Contrasts*, Andre Deutsch, 2002

Interviews

The Princess Who Never Knew Her Place, Selina Hastings, *The Sunday Telegraph*, 1986
Letters from Gore Vidal to Louis Auchincloss, *New Yorker*, 1996
What the Driver Saw, Angelique Chrisafis, *The Guardian*, 2002

Websites

www.bbc.co.uk
www.britroyals.com
www.dailymail.co.uk
www.eonline.com
www.express.co.uk
www.facebook.com/TheBritishMonarchy
www.famousquotesandauthors.com
www.guardian.co.uk
www.huffingtonpost.com
www.independent.co.uk
www.inews.co.uk
www.itv.com
www.lrb.co.uk
www.mirror.co.uk
news.sky.com/uk
www.newstatesman.com
www.newsweek.com

BIBLIOGRAPHY

www.newyorker.com

www.nybooks.com

www.nytimes.com

www.radiotimes.com

uk.reuters.com

www.royal.uk

www.standard.co.uk

www.thesun.co.uk

www.telegraph.co.uk

www.thedailybeast.com

www.thinkexist.com

www.time.com

www.timesonline.co.uk

www.vanityfair.com

www.wikipedia.org

www.youtube.com